THE GODDESS IN CRETE

—

A guide to 100 Minoan and other sites

Cheryl Straffon & Lana Jarvis

Dor Dama Press
(Meyn Mamvro Publications)

The Goddess in Crete –
a guide to 100 Minoan and other sites

by Cheryl Straffon & Lana Jarvis

First Published 2015
Published by Dor Dama Press (Meyn Mamvro Publications)
51 Carn Bosavern, St.Just, Penzance,
Cornwall TR19 7QX

Website: www.meynmamvro.co.uk/dordama

Printed by: Lightning Source

ISBN: 978 0 9518859 9 4

The Author
Cheryl Straffon is author of the following books:-
The Earth Goddess [Blandford, 1997]
Fentynyow Kernow: in search of Cornwall's Holy Wells
    [Meyn Mamvro, 1998/2005]
Megalithic Mysteries of Cornwall [Meyn Mamvro, 2004]
Daughters of the Earth [O Books, 2007]
Pagan Cornwall – Land of the Goddess [Meyn Mamvro, 1993/2012]
Between the Realms: Cornish myth and magic [Troy Books, 2014]
She is also author and compiler of 4 Guides to ancient sites in Cornwall & Scilly, and editor of two magazines: "Meyn Mamvro" and "Goddess Alive!".

Cheryl and Lana live in west Cornwall and also have a home in Crete. They organise Goddess tours to Crete on a regular basis.
www.goddess-tours-international.com
Cover photograph: Invoking the Goddess at Pyrgos, eastern Crete.

CONTENTS

1

BOXED FEATURES

INTRODUCTION

Crete is a very special island. The first settlers arrived here (from Anatolia, modern Turkey) some time after 7000 BCE. From 3500 BCE (the Bronze Age) a completely unique people, one that we now call the Minoans, developed a civilisation that is now world famous. There are many books and Internet sites devoted to that civilisation, and Crete receives thousands of visitors each year, keen to see the sites and soak up its culture. Although there are many published guides to Crete, it seemed to us that what was lacking was a concise Guide to all the archaeological sites that showed exactly what was there, how to get to it, what finds were made, and where they can now be seen. Not an easy task, as some sites are difficult to find, and some finds are not easy to track down. This book attempts to fill that gap, and to also look at the pre-Minoan, Minoan and post-Minoan sites through the lens of Goddess research and reclamation. For one of the reasons that makes the culture so special is that the people seem to have had a deep and abiding love of a Goddess, who infused all the ways that they lived their lives. The extent of that Goddess culture can be argued over - and frequently is in many books and journals; but what cannot be denied is its existence and presence.

We have a close relationship with Crete, and have a house in the southern part of the island. We have spent many enjoyable hours seeking out all the sites in this book, and browsing through the Museums. We have also read as much as we can on the culture and civilisation that formed ancient Crete. We believe that we have included all the sites linked to ancient Crete that most visitors would want to see, and we have also included background information on the culture and civilisation in boxed entries spread throughout the book. Wherever any particular site makes reference to a cultural or religious feature, we have cross-referenced it to one of the boxed entries for ease of consulting. Wherever an entry notes another place or site we have placed it in **bold print**, so that by consulting the Index, the reader can easily find the relevant place or site. Where we have included reference to finds from the site, we have consulted at least two independent sources, as some information that can be read elsewhere about sites and finds is quite contradictory. We have however deliberately not included information about entry to sites (except Museums). This is because it changes all the time. One year a site can be open, with or without a guardian; the next year it can be closed. Some closed sites can be accessed through holes in the fencing, some are impenetrable. Sometimes you can see a site from outside the fencing, sometimes not. Some of the sites featured are on everyone's itinerary; others are remote and isolated and you can probably have the site all to yourself. Take a chance and be prepared for anything!

A couple of final points: [1] The main sites, such as Knossos, Phaistos, Malia and Zakros, are traditionally referred to as 'palaces'. That description has been shown to be inaccurate and inadequate, so we refer to them throughout as 'palace-temples'. And [2] the Greek alphabet and Greek letters do not coincide with English ones, so the same place may have different spellings *(e.g, Chania, Hania and Khania)*. We have chosen what seems to us the most sensible spellings in each case, but be aware there may be others. Please let us know if you find any errors or mistakes, or you discover something that we have not mentioned. We are always pleased to hear from readers.

We hope that you enjoy the sites and the rich culture and wonderful atmosphere of Crete. Between us, we have been visiting Crete for over 30 years and seen many changes during that time. But that is a pinprick of time set against the millennia which constituted the great Minoan culture and its aftermath. We hope that this book will provide at least a taste of that culture and whet your appetite to see the remains of some of the sites that gave rise to this great civilisation.

WHO WERE THE MINOANS?

The name 'Minoan' was given to the people by Sir Arthur Evans, who uncovered and excavated Knossos and other sites at the turn of the 20th century. He based it on the later legend of King Minos who ruled in Crete, but that was not the name that the people used to refer to themselves. We do not know precisely what they called themselves, but a clue may perhaps be found in a wall painting from Thebes in Egypt, dating from 1520-1420 BCE.

This depicts various foreign emissaries coming to give tribute and gifts. Among these are shown the 'Keftiu', who, from their appearance and the goods they are bearing (including ingots, amphorae, engraved jars of gold and silver, and bulls head rhytons) can be confidently assigned to Minoan Crete and dated to the Late Minoan IA period [1550-1500 BCE]. They are named as being "from the land of Keftiu and the islands of the Green Sea".

CRETE – Overview of periods

BCE = Before current era   CE = Current era [AD]

NEOLITHIC [7000 - 3500 BCE]. Evidence of Neolithic occupation has been found all over the island. DNA evidence shows that the first settlers probably arrived from Anatolia and the Middle East, and made extensive use of cave sites (for example at Miamou, Stavomyti at **Mt.Juktas, Gerani**, and **Pelekita**). There was an early Neolithic settlement at **Knossos** on the Kephali Hill, where cereal crops were grown and animals domesticated. One of the finest Goddess figurines comes from this period, found at **Kato Horio**, and now in the Heraklion Archaeological Museum.

BRONZE AGE [3500 - 970 BCE]. The Bronze Age in Crete is divided into a number of periods that encompass the full flowering of the Minoan people. The designations were originally given by Sir Arthur Evans as Early Minoan (EM), Middle Minoan (MM) and Late Minoan (LM). These periods were further subdivided by numbers and then by letters. Subsequently, a more simplified system was devised, divided into Prepalatial, Protopalatial, Neopalatial and Postpalatial, which is what this book uses, with Evans' designations added in brackets.

[1] - PREPALATIAL [3500 - 1900 BCE], including EM I, II & III and MM IA. It has been recently shown that the Prepalatial people were descendants of their Neolithic ancestors, and not a completely new people, though there may have been further arrivals from Anatolia as well. People began to settle more extensively at places such as **Phourni Korphi** and **Vasiliki**, which gave its name to the pottery associated with this period. Metalworking was discovered, and many fine objects in copper, bronze, silver and gold were made. Cemeteries came into use, such as **Phourni** (near Archanes), **Mochlos** and the **Mesara Plain**. A Goddess of nature and nurture was celebrated and depicted in items such as libation jugs and Cycladic-style figurines.

[2] - PROTOPALATIAL [1900 - 1700 BCE], including MMIB & MMII.
This was the Old Palace period and saw the first palace-temple sites of **Knossos, Phaistos, Malia** and **Zakros** being built. Economy flourished, and there was trade with overseas places. A new style of pottery was developed, called Kamares ware, and seal stones were engraved that depicted the Goddess in a natural environment. Religion was now organised through the palace-temple sites and the Peak Sanctuaries, and focussed on a vegetation Goddess of the seasons and the cycles of life, death and regeneration. The bee goddess pendant from **Malia** comes from this period. Around 1700 BCE there was a severe earthquake that destroyed sites.

[3] - NEOPALATIAL [1700 - 1450 BCE], including MMIII & LMI.
After the 1700 BCE severe earthquake that destroyed most of the palace-temple sites, they were rebuilt, often to a greater complexity, and town houses and countryside villas, such as **Tylissos** and **Makriyalos** were constructed. This New Palace Temple period is the era of the full flowering of the rich Minoan culture in all its beauty, and full details may be found on pages 11-20. It paints a vivid picture of how religious life and celebration of the Goddess underpinned and permeated every aspect of society and everyday living. Minoan colonies were established on islands such as Kythera and Thera (Santorini).
Around 1630-1600 BCE the volcanic island of Thera erupted, and the subsequent tsunami undoubtedly caused serious damage to coastal settlements. It may also have weakened the political structure, but it was not until 1450 BCE that a devastating fire and conflagration swept through the island, destroying most of the Minoan sites, though **Knossos** continued in use for a further 150 years. The causes of this conflagration are not properly known, but the results were devastating.

[4] - POSTPALATIAL [1450 - 1100 BCE], including LMII & LMIII.
The consequence of the 1450 BCE conflagration was that Mycenean people from the Greek mainland now arrived on the island and seemed to have taken over, rebuilt and re-occupied some of the buildings. However, contrary to some misunderstandings, this did not mean the end of Goddess worship on the island. Although there is little evidence for it on the Mycenean mainland, here on Crete they seem to have combined their culture with the Minoan one, and produced large numbers of GUAs (Goddesses with Upraised Arms) and other sacred objects.

[5] - SUBMINOAN [1100 - 970 BCE]. This period saw the last of Minoan people fleeing to refuge sites such as **Karphi, Vrokastro, Kastro, Azorias, Praisos** and **Syvritos**, as new invaders, such as the Dorians, arrived on the island. However, the people did not abandon their Goddess faith, and figurines and votive offerings have been found at these sites.

IRON AGE [970 - 67 BCE]. This encompasses the Geometric & Orientalising periods [970-650 BCE] and the Archaic, Classical and Hellenistic periods [650-67 BCE]. The period saw the rise of the City States, and a more public side to worship. Goddesses were still invoked and celebrated (some of whom may have descended directly from the Minoan Goddess of nature *see p.31-2*), and it is from this period that we have the first named Goddesses *[see box on p.32 for more details]*. Gods too were also worshipped. These City States did flourish during this period, but were themselves conquered by the Romans in 67 BCE under a Roman general who named himself 'Creticus'. Minoan Crete was now a memory.

CENTRAL CRETE [Heraklion province] – map

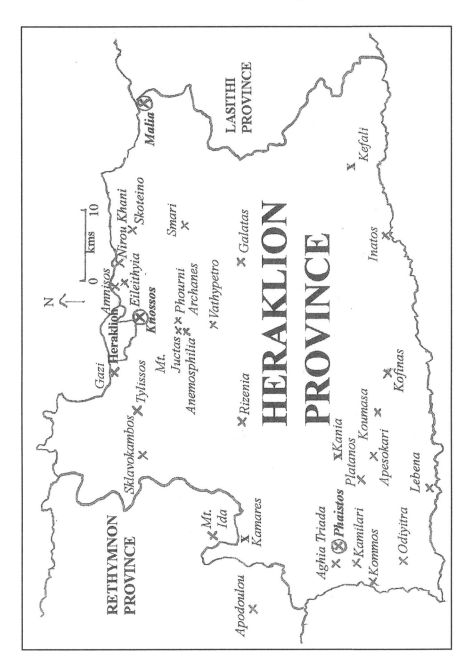

CENTRAL CRETE
[Province of Heraklion]

The area of Central Crete encompasses the capital city of Crete, Heraklion with its Archaeological Museum; the world-famous Minoan palace-temple sites of Knossos, Malia and Phaistos; the sacred mountains of Mt. Jucktas; the cemetery of Phourni and the tholos tombs of the Mesara Plain; major settlement sites at Archanes and Aghia Triada; the temple shrine of Anemosphilia; the sacred caves of Skoteino and Eileithyia; houses at Tylissos, Zominthos and Apodoulou; the port at Kommos; a recently discovered settlement at Galatas and villas such as Vathypetro, Amnisos, Nirou and Sklavokambos. This is an archaeologically rich area, and many superb Minoan Goddess-inspired finds have come from here.

HERAKLION

This capital city of Crete has a long history. There is evidence of Neolithic occupation on the high ground above the Kairatos stream bed to the east of the present town. The Minoans had a harbour here, known as Katsambas (in the modern suburb of Poros). Then the Romans had a port hereabouts, called Heracleum. The Arabs (Saracens) occupied it from 827-961 CE, followed by the Venetians, who developed it and called it Candia. It was under Turkish rule from 1667, and not re-named Heraklion until 1898. In 1914 Crete was finally united with Greece, but it was not until 1971 that it became the capital of the island.

ARCHAEOLOGICAL MUSEUM

Open: Daily 0800-2000 (Mondays 1300-2000).
Sundays & public holidays 0800-1500.
Location: on Odos Hatzidakis, just off the Platia Eleftherias, which lies just inside the city walls, not far from the harbour and the main bus station.

After being closed for a number of years for renovation, the Museum re-opened fully in 2014. It has been beautifully refurbished, with extensive marble throughout. There are eight rooms on the Ground Floor, displaying artefacts from the Neolithic and Bronze Age (Prepalatial, Protopalatial, Neopalatial and Postpalatial) periods, together with detailed information plaques that provide the background to the Minoan culture and civilisation. On the First Floor is a room that displays the Minoan frescos, and other rooms covering later periods, such as the Geometric, Archaic, Classical, Hellenistic and Iron Age periods. Allow plenty of time to fully savour the treasures that are on show in the Museum.

Guide to the Museum

Ground Floor
1st room: Neolithic 7000-3000 BCE

The Neolithic period marked the earliest settlers in Crete, and the establishment of the first settlements, particularly at **Knossos**. Artefacts from this period include pottery in dark burnished wares, sometimes with decoration of simple geometric patterns, stone and bone tools, bone arrowheads, stone vessels and maceheads. Female figurines from this period have been found, in both stone and clay, the most noteable example of which is the Goddess figurine discovered at **Kato Horio**, north of Irepetra in southern Crete.

Kato Horio Goddess

Prepalatial 3000-1900 BCE

Jug with horns

Settlements continued to grow, most notably at **Phourni Korphi** (Myrtos) and **Vasiliki**. This expansion was fuelled in part by the discovery of metalworking, in particular of copper, but also bronze, silver and gold. The wide variety of gold jewellery, using advanced techniques such as granulation and filigree, forms the largest collection of its kind in prehistoric Aegean during this period. Silver and bronze daggers, figurines and seal-amulets, elaborate stone vessels and clay amulets all bear witness to the craftsmanship and artistic imagination of their makers. Most figurines, made of stone or bone, are in the shape of women and/or Goddesses. They have been found in tombs, and many show links with the Cycladic islands. The Museum has examples of many of these Goddess and zoomorphic figurines, and also examples of Vasiliki ware *[see box on p.10]* cups with spirals, and cases of seal imprints and stones, and gold wire and faience necklaces.

Cycladic-style figurines

2nd room: Prepalatial 3000-1900 BCE (cont.)

This room continues the late Prepalatial period with information on Life in the Settlements (for example **Malia**) and finds from the cemeteries (for example **Phourni** near Archanes). Exhibits include jugs and offering tables, (such as Goddess libation jugs, found at **Mochlos** and other places), Cycladic-type Goddess figurines, bulls heads, animal parts, and models of male and female adorants, found at Peak Sanctuaries *[see box on p.16]* and other shrines. Note the model of a bull with tiny acrobats clinging to its horns, which was found in a **Mesara tomb**. Clearly the ritual significance of bulls and bull leaping finds its origins in this early period before its manifestation at Knossos later. These Mesara tombs were in use for many generations in this period, and some continued into the Protopalatial period.

Libation vessels (from Mochlos right)

Goddess adorants

MINOAN POTTERY. The earliest form of Minoan pottery is **Vasiliki ware**, named after the site in Eastern Crete, which dates from the Prepalatial period. It has a distinctive mottled or patterned surface achieved by burnishing with uneven firing, and decoration that consists of narrow stripes of red or brown on a buff or cream background.

By the Protopalatial period potters had discovered the use of a fast potters wheel that enabled the production of fine polychrome vases, known as **Kamares ware**, named after the cave where it was first discovered on the flanks of **Mount Ida** in western Crete. The quality and range of the ware is outstanding, ranging from delicate thin-walled vases, to bridge-spouted jars and containers, to large pots (pithoi). They are often decorated with spirals, whorls and other patterns that resemble faces and eyes, which have been interpreted as forms and features of the Goddess.

Kamares ware

Protopalatial 1900-1700 BCE

The Protopalatial period marks the rise of the first palace-temple sites, and there is information in this room on Kamares Ware pottery *[see box on p.10]*, writing and economic administration (the earliest Cretan script, heiroglyphic appears for the first time in this period) *[see box on p12]*, weapons and authority symbols, and the cult in palaces and settlements.

Bee Goddess from Malia

Amongst the exhibits are Kamares ware bowls and jugs, and two superb artefacts found at **Malia**, the bee-goddess pendant (from Chrysolakkos), and the leopard or panther axe sceptre. There is also mention of the finds from the palace-temple site at **Phaistos**, including cult vessels, such as offering tables, a concave altar, human and animal vessels and figurines. On an altar and bowl are depicted the first known epiphany scenes *[see box on p.18]*, in

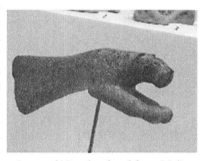

Leopard / Panther head from Malia

which the Goddess miraculously appears in the human world. The divine image, or a priestess with a flower, are shown between groups of dancing women. The scene is a reference to the Goddess' attribute of rendering nature fertile.

3rd room: Neopalatial 1700-1450 BCE

The next 4 rooms (rooms 3-6) have material from the finest flowering of the Minoan culture, the Neopalatial period. This room has information on the New Palaces, architecture, central buildings and settlements, harbours, miniature art, and international commerce and cultural influences. From the palace and town of **Knossos** objects of exceptional quality are displayed They were produced by specialised workshops, and included stone lamps and vessels with elaborate relief

Marine style pottery

decoration, bronze vessels, and elegant vases with raised pictorial compositions or inlaid and covered in fine gold leaf, with subjects from the vegetable (Floral Style) and sea world (Marine Style).

3rd room: Neopalatial 1700-1450 BCE (cont.)

During this period Minoan artists produced art in gold, silver and ivory, with motifs from the worlds of land, sea and sky. Among the artefacts in this room is a beautiful game board from **Knossos** inlaid with rock crystals, glass paste and lapis lazuli, decorated with gold and silver leaf. There are also pots of the

Pots showing an octopus & a butterfly / double axe

Marine Style, and one showing a butterfly evolving into a double axe symbol *[see box on p.14]*. In the display cases there are scripts and sealing practices, including Linear A seals *[see box below]*, a Minoan system of weights, and the famous Phaistos Disk.

MINOAN SCRIPT. The oldest form of Minoan script were **hieroglyphs**, developed from Egyptian sources. This script has been found on clay bars, sealings and labels, where it was used for labelling and counting. It appears for the first time on seals with pictograms from **Phourni** in 1900 BCE, and has also been found at **Knossos, Phaistos, Malia** and **Petras**. This system was superseded by **Linear A** script, which may have developed from it. Linear A was used at the old palace-temple sites, and also other places such as **Aghia Triada, Tylissos, Palaikastro** and **Myrtos**. Linear A has never been properly deciphered, though on one tablet the name of a Goddess, Assassara, has been identified, making her the earliest, and probably least-known of any Minoan Goddess. **Linear B** as a script was developed at the end of the Neopalatial period, and, although many of the signs are identical or similar to those of Linear A, it appears to be a different language (early Greek). An archive of Linear B texts was discovered at **Knossos**, having been baked during the conflagration of 1450 BCE. This script continued to be used during the Postpalatial period by the Myceneans at **Knossos, Hania** and other sites, and on the mainland. The greatest collection of 3400 items was found at Knossos (dated to 1425-1300 BCE), and it was deciphered by Michael Ventris in 1953. Amongst the Linear B words, which could possibly be Goddess names are: 'po-ti-ni-ja-we-jo/ja' = Potnia ("The Lady Aphrodite"?); 'a-ta-na-po-ti-ni-ja' ("The Lady Athena"?); 'e-ri-nu' = Erinys (Demeter?); 'pi-pi-tu-na' = Pipituna (an unknown moon Goddess); 'a-pe-ti-ra' = the bow Goddess (Athena?); 'qe-ra-si-ja' = the huntress (Athena?); and 'a-ne-mo' = the priestess of the winds.

The Phaistos Disc (found at **Phaistos** temple-palace site in southern Crete in 1908) is a circular clay tablet which is roughly 15cm (6in) in diameter, and is dated to the second millenium BCE. It has symbols stamped on both sides, written in a spiral pattern, that was intended to be read from the outside in. The disc includes 242 picture segments from 45 individual symbols, many of which represent everyday things. Many theories have been advanced as to the meaning of the symbols, but recently a team of researchers, led by Dr. Gareth Owens of the Technological

Phaistos Disc

Educational Institute of Crete, have claimed to have deciphered 90% of the symbols on side A, and say that the most important one is a picture segment that shows a plumed head, a circular object with 5 circles around a central one, a bird, and a curved stick. This picture segment is repeated three times on one side of the disc, and spells out I-QE-KU-RJA, which Owens believes means "Great lady of importance" or the Mother Goddess of the Minoan era. He adds that the symbols on the disc are very like the language of Linear A script, which has only been partially deciphered, but which can be used to throw light on the symbols of the disc. On the other side of the double-sided disc, he identified the word AKKA, which he says means 'pregnant mother'. Taken together, he believes that the disc is a Minoan prayer to the Mother Goddess.

4th room: Neopalatial 1700-1450 BCE (cont.)
This 4th room continues with the Neopalatial period, and has information on the private and public life of Minoan society, including cooking and eating, production of wine and honey, clothing and ornaments, music and dance, and athletic events. The objects on display in this room include jewel boxes, bronze discs used as mirrors, combs, gaming pieces from board games, objects used for wine production, and musical instruments. The Minoans used music in their dances and processions, and had three kinds of musical instrument: wind instruments, with tritons and aulos pipes; stringed instruments, with lyres and perhaps harps; and percussion instruments, with cymbals and sistrums. There is also information on bull-leaping, in which young, trained athletes, both male and female, made a dangerous leap over the horns and back of a charging bull. This bull-leaping spectacle is depicted on a series of wall paintings *[see p.28]* and gold rings and seals, and may have been part of a ceremonial activity, in which the sacredness of the bull was recognised by participants and spectators alike. It may well be that the horns of the bull became stylized into horns of consecration *[see box on p.15]*.

4th room: Neopalatial 1700-1450 BCE (cont.)

In the corner of the room are three full-sized double-axes, from the site at **Knossos**, which are attached to modern stands *[photo in box below]*.

THE DOUBLE-AXE or to give it its Greek name, the labrys, has become one of the most potent symbols of Minoan Crete, and in modern times adapted by feminists and lesbians. It appears in 'masons marks' on the walls of some of the rooms at **Knossos, Malia** and **Zakros**, on pots and sculptures from all periods of Minoan and Mycenean history, in exquisite necklaces and personal objects, and as miniature objects given as votive offerings in some of the sacred caves in Crete, most notably the **Dicktean** and **Arkalochori** caves. It was clearly a well understood symbol, widely used in a sacred context, and in everyday use. When it is used in an everyday context (such as the 'masons marks'

on walls of a building), it may have been placed there to show the sacred nature of the room. Nanno Marinatos says: "It is plausible that the purpose of such signs would be to impart a magico-religious meaning to utilitarian structures". The problem for us today is that there is no written explanation from this time as to its actual meaning. However, there is a bronze axe that was found in the Arkalochori cave from the Neopalatial period, which had been left as a votive offering, that has an inscription arranged in three columns running down the central socket of the axe, that has certain signs similar to the Phaistos Disc *[see p.13]*, while others resemble linear A signs *[see box on p.12]*, all of which indicate that it has a sacred meaning. There is some evidence that the stylized double axe arose from depictions of a butterfly *[see p.12 & p.99]* which would make it a symbol of nature and gentleness, not warfare and power-wielding. In addition, Minoan seals show axes being carried by women, and a Postpalatial mold from **Palaikastro** shows two double axes displayed by a Goddess. The **Aghia Triada** Sarcophagus *[see page 24-5]* also shows a scene of an altar between two pillared labyrises, in front of which is a priestess pouring libations. Its most common depiction is in contexts where ritual took place – for example double-axe stands have been found in crypts at **Knossos**, in House A at **Tylissos**, and the temple tomb of Isopata at **Knossos**. We can thus infer that it was a symbol of ceremony and ritual to honour or represent the Goddess.

5th room: Neopalatial 1700-1450 BCE – Minoan Religion

The next two rooms – Rooms 5 & 6 – are perhaps the most important for the study of the religious beliefs and practices of Minoan society at the height of the Palace-Temple period. In this room there is information on domestic and open-air cults, caves, open air sanctuaries and Peak Sanctuaries, figurines and libation vessels, domestic shrines and cult vessels and religious imagery. It talks about how small shrines in houses and peripheral administrative complexes served the

needs of the family and wider community, and how open-air worship also continued at certain Peak Sanctuaries and in caves. Amongst the ritual objects on display in this room are horns of consecration, gold and silver miniature double-axes, votive offerings, cult vessels, figures in salutation, and clay models of religious images. All together, they paint a vivid picture of how religious life in Minoan times underpinned and permeated every aspect of society and everyday living.

Horns of Consecration

HORNS OF CONSECRATION. Along with the Double Axe *[see page 14]* Horns of Consecration are among the most ubiquitous religious symbols of Minoan Religion. The symbol may be found in frescos, on seal stones, in pottery, and adorning public buildings (most notably at **Knossos** *[see page 36]*). Since it is usually found in sacred contexts, its meaning is presumed to relate to worship of a deity, the Goddess. Because of the bull cult in Minoan Crete, it has been suggested that the horns originally arose as a stylized version of the horns of the bull. The connection to sacred ritual can be found by the use of horns to crown an altar, and with a space for a bough or double axe placed between them. The depiction of horns of consecration in many wall paintings and frescos is extensive. For example, one miniature painting

from **Knossos** shows a tripartite shrine crowned with 15 horns of consecration above, and several below *[photo right]*. A stone rhyton from **Zakros** also depicts a Peak Sanctuary *[see p.110 & box on p.16]* whose walls are topped with a number of horns of consecration. And a model found at the Peak Sanctuary of **Petsophas** is in the shape of two huge sacred horns, one inside the other *[see p.84]*.

The next display in this room is from the **Arkalochori** Cave in central Crete (no longer accessible), and features a large collection of metal objects, used for religious rites and votive offerings. This includes copper ingots, numerous bronze model swords and daggers, large bronze votive double axes, and a wealth of miniature double axes in gold, silver and bronze, together with pieces of gold foil. There is also an inscribed double axe with symbols similar to those on the Phaistos Disc *[see p.13 and box on p.14]*.

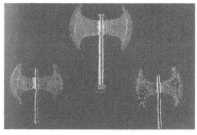

Gold axes from the Arkalochori cave

The next display features Open-Air Sanctuaries and Peak Sanctuaries, with examples of votive offerings from many of the Peak Sanctuaries.

PEAK SANCTUARIES. Peak Sanctuaries are a notable feature of Minoan religious life. They began in the Protopalatial period and continued into the Neopalatial. Although located on summits of mountains, they were not too far away from settlements and could be easily reached from there. Finds from excavated sites (such as **Mount Jucktas** and **Petsophas**) have yielded a wealth of finds. These include bronze and clay figurines, offering tables, gold and bronze objects, jewellery and seals, which were presumably given as offerings to the Goddess at the altars that exist at these sites. Some of these objects are obviously luxury items, emblems of the official religion, but there are many other, more modest gifts, such as lumps of clay moulded into various shapes, indicating that the sites were used by everyone. Animal figurines abound: oxen, sheep and goats are very common, but there are also dogs, cats, hedgehogs, tortoises, weasels, birds, fish and snakes. All this shows that the Goddess worshipped at these places was primarily a Goddess of nature, or 'Lady of the Beasts' as she is sometimes called. In addition to the depictions of animals and birds, there are also figurines, including birthing or nursing mothers (akourotrophos), and parts of the body, presumably deposited with an apotropaic intent. The Peak Sanctuaries are always located in high places amongst the natural environment of rocks and trees, and the one on **Mount Jucktas** has a deep natural rock chasm into which offerings were thrown. Peak Sanctuaries were therefore important places to which people would make pilgrimages and offer gifts to the Goddess *[see also p.107 & 110]*.

5th room: Neopalatial 1700-1450 BCE – Minoan Religion (cont.)

Finally in the 5th room, there is information and displays about domestic shrines *[see box on p.98]*, with figurines and libation vessels. Many such figurines and cult vessels have been found, mainly from **Aghia Triada** and **Kania** near Gortyn. The figurines depict acts of worship, including a seated figure (perhaps a Goddess or a

Goddess in shrine (left) & Goddess-style jug (right)

priestess), figures in dancing postures, making gestures of invocation to the Goddess, and a Goddess in a shrine with horns of consecration *[photo above left]*. There are also rhyton (libation vessels) in conical, egg-shaped and bulls head shapes, and triton shells for pouring liquid offerings. The vase *[photo above right]* has an upper Goddess shape with raised breast-like bosses. There are offering tables, upon which were placed small quantities of fruit or grain, while the stone conical bases supported the shafts of double axes. These exquisite objects show a society that expended time and effort in creating beautiful gifts for the Goddess.

6th room: Neopalatial 1700-1450 BCE – Minoan Religion (cont.)

Minoan religion continues in this room with a look at Palace-Temple cults. The information unequivocally states that Minoan religious belief was expressed in the worship of the Great Goddess, protectress of nature, with a male figure, the escort or companion of the Goddess, as a secondary figure. The Minoan religious worldview was that the cohesion and stability of the natural world were ensured by the divine powers of the Goddess. Large communal religious ceremonies were held in the halls and in open-air spaces of the Palace-Temple sites, in particular in the central and west courts. Most of the exhibits in this room relate to this public side of Minoan worship, in particular seal stones, libation vessels, ritual vases; and the Temple Repositries and sacred objects discovered at the Palace-Temple sites of **Knossos** and **Zakros**, with particular focus on the Snake Goddess / Priestess figurines found at **Knossos**.

6th room: Neopalatial 1700-1450 BCE – Minoan Religion (cont.)
Examples of gold, silver and bronze rings are shown, including some from **Knossos, Zakros, Mochlos, Aghia Triada** and the **Idean Cave**. Two of these seal rings are famous for showing scenes of a Goddess epiphany. The 'Ring of Minos' was found in 1923/4 at Knossos, disappeared from circulation, and only recently (2002) has been acquired by the Museum; and 'The descent of the Goddess' ring is from the tomb at Isopata at **Knossos**.

The Ring of Minos   *The Descent of the Goddess*

The EPIPHANY OF THE GODDESS is something that was enacted in Minoan Crete, and continues to fascinate today. Described as "the vision of a deity and her descent to the visible world" and "the appearance of a living Goddess", there are two possible ways that this might have happened. One is by appearing to the worshipper in some kind of ecstatic vision. This is what seems to have been depicted on both the rings illustrated above. On 'The Ring of Minos' two worshippers are shown adoring trees, on the left a female and in the centre a male. On the right, a Goddess is shown hovering in the air before descending on to a throne prepared for her. Her downward movement is denoted conventionally by the fact that her hair waves in the air and by the downward slope of her feet. On the throne are horns of consecration *[see page 15]* which indicate 'deity'. In 'The Descent of the Goddess' ring, the small hovering figure of the Goddess is depicted in the background (top left of the illustration), while four adorants call her down. The main cult rituals connected with the epiphany of the Goddess are tree-worship, in which the sacred tree is shaken by ecstatic devotees, and baetyl-worship, with the embracing of the baetyl, the sacred stone enshrining the divine powers *[see box on p.58]*. The epiphany rites include dancing by groups of women making gestures of invocation to the Goddess. The epiphany cycle may also include a male figure who converses with the Goddess.

The other way that epiphany may have been experienced is by a priestess embodying the Goddess. More details of this are on page 39.

6th room: Neopalatial 1700-1450 BCE – Minoan Religion (cont.)

Also in this room are finds from the temple repositories at the Palace-Temple site of **Knossos**, and in particular the two famous 'Snake Goddesses'. They are made of faience, but were found in a very fragmentary state, amongst gold foil, fragments of worked ivory and rock crystal, bronze and stone implements, numerous bones and shells, and clay sealings, inlays and plaques. When the material was sorted by Evans it became clear that the fragments of at least five faience statuettes had been recovered.

Of the two that have been restored, the most famous one *[photo right above]* had her head and most of her left arm missing. These missing parts (including the snake) were fashioned and attached by Halvor Bagge, a Scandinavian artist employed by Evans. The crouching feline (cat?) on her head is original, though it was not found with the statuette, but incorporated by Bagge into it. One extant arm was holding a snake, or at least a possible snake, but its head was missing and was also fashioned by Bagge.

The second figure *[photo right below]* with undulating serpents knotted at her waist framing her bare breasts, was also restored by Bagge. She was found only preserved to the hips, and the lower portion is entirely modern and was based on the remnants of a third statuette with horizontally flounced skirt and decorated apron. Her neck, most of her face and the snake's head on top of her headdress are also modern. Although they are often shown equal in size, in fact the second figure *[below]* is larger than the first one *[above]*. Evans suggested that the one below was a Goddess, whilst the one above was a Priestess. Others have suggested Mother and Daughter, but neither explanation seems likely. The reality is that they are probably just two (restored) figurines from a number found in the same place. There are no other examples of figurines with snakes from elsewhere in this Neopalatial period, so it seems likely that these represent a cult that was practised at Knossos to do with the Priestess of the Temple invoking serpent energy, and embodying the Goddess. Perhaps they should more accurately be described as 'Snake energy Priestesses'.

6th room: Neopalatial 1700-1450 BCE – Minoan Religion (cont.)

Other treasures featured in this room include rhytons (libation vessels), including the Bull's Head Rhyton from the **Little Palace at Knossos** *[right]*. This superby-crafted libation jug is carved from sepentine, with eyes inlaid with jasper and rock crystal. The horns (which are restored) were made of gilded wood. There are holes in the mouth and crown of the head for pouring libations, and there is a double axe carved between the eyes. This piece is further evidence of the bull cult at Knossos.

Bull's Head rhyton

There are three more rhytons of exceptional quality on display in the Museum. One, from the west wing Upper Halls of **Knossos**, is the rhyton in the form of a lioness's head (or leopard's head), made of off-white translucent alabaster *[photo right]*. The inlays in the snout and eyes, possibly of jasper and crystal, like those on the bull's head rhyton, have not been preserved, but it is still a lovely piece.

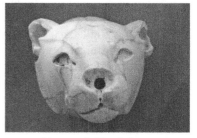

Lionesse's Head rhyton

The second rhyton is the Harvester Vase rhyton from **Aghia Triada**, which has only the upper half preserved. It depicts a harvest procession of youths, with the leader carrying a long rod, and the others pitchforks and scythes. They are accompanied by four singers, one of which is a sistrum player.

The third rhyton is the rock-crystal rhyton from the palace-temple site at **Zakros** *[photo right]*, an exquisite piece, reconstructed from hunderds of tiny fragments. It has an elongated body with pointed bottom made of an unusually large piece of rock crystal. The neck and splaying rim, also of rock crystal, are joined to the body by a crystal ring decorated with vertical rings of gilt faience. The tall handle is formed by fourteen beads of gilt crystal, threaded onto a bronze wire. A superb example of Minoan craft work.

Rock crystal rhyton

7th room: Final Palatial period at Knossos 1450-1300 BCE

Although 1450 BCE marks the end of the Neopalatial period throughout the rest of Crete following the conflagration that swept through the island, at Knossos the Palace-Temple site was rebuilt and continued in use for a further 150 years, perhaps under Mycenean management. This is now called in the Museum "The Knossos Monopalatial system", and is featured in this 7th room. Amongst the items on display are clay tablets inscribed in the 'new' Linear B script *[see box on p.12]*, which are mainly lists of commodities, but also give names of some Goddesses, who may be the foremothers of the polytheistic Goddesses and Gods of the later Greek pantheon. The Museum reproduces a record of wool produced from the flocks of the Goddess Potnia.

There is also information on cemeteries and monumental tombs. In the Neopalatial period most tombs were excavated at **Poros**, the harbour of **Knossos**, but many more were found dating to this Final Palace period. These are mainly found at **Knossos, Poros & Katsambos, Phourni** and near **Phaistos**. They consist of rock-cut chamber tombs, shaft graves with side chambers and several tholos tombs *[see p.44-47]*. The 'Royal Tomb' at Isopata (Knossos) and the 'Temple Tomb' at Knossos, in the form of a house and stoa (a free-standing colonnaded portico), were monumental structures. There is a clay model of a stoa on display in this room. So-called 'Warrior Graves' at **Knossos** are also featured, These were burials with many weapons, mostly swords and spears, as well as boar's-tusk and bronze helmets. These may be evidence of conflict at this time between the Minoan people and the incoming Mycenean invaders. Many burials were accompanied by rich grave offerings, including high-status gold jewellery, and in this room are displayed gold and amber necklaces from the tombs at **Phourni** *[photo right]*. It also mentions the rock-cut Tomb of the Tripod Hearth at **Knossos** from this period that contained a wealth of grave goods relating to ritual feasting, including an intact tripod cauldron, a small cauldron, a bronze washbowl, three lamps and vessels for making liquid offerings.

The room also displays several burial pithoi (vases) and larnakes (stone coffins).

Gold and amber necklaces from Phourni

8th room: Postpalatial 1300-1100 BCE

The Postpalatial period in Cretan history is covered in this 8th and final room on the Ground Floor. There is information on settlements, shrines, cemeteries, and in particular the figurines known as Goddesses with Upraised Arms (GUAs). Settlement during this period conisted of reoccupation of some Minoan buildings, but there was also new development at places such as **Aghia Triada** and **Tylissos**. The centre of power shifted further west to **Hania**, where the town developed rapidly. Peripheral cemeteries have been found at places such as Agios Silas, south of Knossos. Burials were in wooden coffins and on biers, and were accompanied by weapons and bronze vessels, or in larnakes, some of which are displayed in this room. There is still an ongoing debate about whether the incoming Mycenean people from the mainland conquered the native Minoan people, or whether there was more of a peaceful assimililation. However, many of the remnants of the Minoan people may have moved to new inaccessible mountain refuges, such as **Kefali** (near Hondros), **Karphi, Lato, Vrokastro** and **Kastro** (near Vronda).

Figures of GUAs had pride of place in the communal shrines of the Postpalatial period. The size of the figurines (much larger than the Goddess figurines of the Minoan period) and their placement on raised benches or altars, indicate their importance to these Minoan-Mycenean people as significant religious objects.

Goddesses with Upraised Arms

There is a magnificent display of many of these GUAs in this room, together with fragments of several others, and other ritual implements, such as tubular offering stands and cups. The GUAs come from a variety of different Postpalatial sites, and they appear to have been made by different artists with individual variations around a common theme.

GUAs with ritual implements

22

GODDESSES WITH UPRAISED ARMS (GUAs). These large terracotta Goddess figurines, most of which have cylindrical skirts and upraised arms, have been found at many Postpalatial sites, including **Knossos, Gournia, Ayia Triada, Myrtos, Rizenia, Gazi, and Kania** (near Gortyn). These GUAs are often associated with classic Minoan symbols, such as flowers, birds, snakes and horns of consecration, so the themes of Minoan Goddess sacred worship continued into these later times. Some of the figures have moveable feet, which so far has not been adequately explained. Their meaning is still hotly debated: suggestions include a Goddess as mistress or protectress of nature, a Goddess expressing entreaty on behalf of humankind, or a Goddess accepting the praying worshippers' supplications. It is also possible that they may represent Priestess invocations to the Goddess. There has also been the suggestion that the individual Goddess figurines were dressed with specially made clothes for ceremonial occasions (a mould found at **Roussolakkos** give some weight to this). Nanno Marinatos suggested that each figure represented an individual dedication by an important family or clan in the community. These GUA figurines are unique to Crete, and none have been found on the mainland from where the Myceneans came, so it may well be the Postpalatial Myceneans absorbed some of the Minoan Goddess worship into their culture, or it may be that the Minoan people who remained did not lose their faith in the Goddess, but felt that after the conflagration of 1450 BCE, she needed a larger version of herself to be made to invoke her aid.

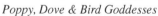

Poppy, Dove & Bird Goddesses   *Snake Goddess from Kania*

From **Gazi** *[photo above left]* comes several figurines. On the left is the Poppy Goddess. This figurine, some 75cm tall, has three poppy heads in her crown, and it has been suggested that this is a reference to the taking of opium to induce trance or sleep in ritual, or as an offering to the dead. In the centre is a Goddess with a dove in her hat, and on the right is one with birds and horns of consecration. From **Kania** *[photo above right]* several more figurines were found. Two figures had snakes on their heads and one had arms entwined with snakes. A similar 'snake GUA' was found at the Postpalatial part of the site at **Gournia**.

8th room: Postpalatial 1300-1100 BCE (cont.)

Also in this room are examples of animal figurines, and snake tubes *[photo right].* These curious ritual objects, found at sites such as **Gournia** and **Koumasa**, were made out of clay and decorated with snake-like loops down the side of the vases. It has been suggested that snakes may actually have been kept in the tubes, but whether they were or not, they are evidence of a probable snake cult, associated with a Snake Goddess.

Snake tubes

The other major artefact on display in this room is the Aghia Triada sarcophagus. This magnificent limestone burial chest was discovered at **Aghia Triada** near Phaistos and dated to the Postpalatial period of about 1400 BCE. It was originally coated in plaster with a frieze depicting vivid scenes of Minoan funerary rites. Both the long sides depict funeral ceremonies, and the ends two Goddesses in chariots.

Nanno Marinatos suggests that taken all together, the two sides and two ends of the sarcophagus are illustrating the cycle of the cult of the dead *[see box on p.47].* On side A there are ceremonies concerned with the disposal of the dead, and the preparations for the journey of the spirit to the next world. On side B there are rituals of renewal for the spirit of the dead, symbolised by a tree as a focal point. The two ends show on one *[photo right above]* two chthonic Goddesses in a chariot drawn by wild goats, who are travelling towards the scene on side A. On the other ***[photo right below]*** it shows two celestial Goddesses in a chariot drawn by griffins *[see box on p.101],* travelling towards the shrine on side B. Full details of the scenes on sides A & B are on the next page.

Side A *[illustrated above]* has two scenes showing processions of figures bearing offerings. On the left a female figure pours the contents of a vase into a large two-handled bowl. She is obviously conducting a purification rite for the deceased. Behind her is another woman in a long robe wearing a crown (priestess?) who is carrying two more vessels containing liquid for the libation. Behind her, a man dressed in a long robe is playing a seven string lyre. There are also two full-sized double axes with birds perching on them, empasising the sacred nature of the scene. On the right, a procession of men conveys gifts, including a model boat, towards a figure in front of a richly decorated building. This figure may be a representation of the spirit of the deceased, with the boat being brought for his journey to the next world.

On Side B *[illustrated above]* priestesses are shown officiating at the sacrifice of a trussed bull, to an accompaniment on a flute. A shrine is depicted, topped by two pairs of two sacred horns, between which stands a small olive tree. In front of the shrine is a pole with a double axe, with a bird perched on top. To the left is a smaller altar on which stands a bowl. Above it is a pitcher and a basket of fruit. In front of the small altar a priestess stands with her palms facing downwards, indicating that this is a sacrifice to the chthonic Goddess of the earth. Behind her a bull is being sacrificed, accompanied by a man playing a flute, and behind him another priestess leads a procession of more women.

This beautiful sarcophagus, rich with religious imagery, completes the rooms on the Ground Floor of the Museum.

Guide to the Museum

First Floor.
Room 1. Minoan frescos.

FRESCOS or Minoan wall paintings first appeared during the Prepalatial period, around 1800 BCE. They flourished in the middle of the second millennium BCE (Protopalatial and Neopalatial periods), and fell into decline after the destruction of **Knossos** 1350-1300 BCE. They were a visually rich and vibrant depiction of secular and religious life in Minoan times, with scenes from the palace-temples, such as Knossos, and also from the world of nature. Religious rituals are depicted, thought to revolve around the worship of a Minoan Goddess, and many of the priestesses, officials and supplicants involved in those rituals are depicted (the women drawn in white and the men in brown). It is primarily women who are depicted in these frescos, either as priestesses or women of the 'Court'. From the world of nature (probably illustrating the Goddess of the natural world and all its creatures) come drawings of flora and fauna, including lilies, roses, myrtle, crocuses, wild goats, partridges and other birds, wildcats, dolphins, fish, octupi, and even exotic monkeys, sacred to the Goddess. These creatures are shown in gardens and rivers, on rocky mountainsides and in marine environments.

The frescos were painted by applying pigments to fresh plaster when it was wet. These pigments were earthen, mineral, organic and artificial, such as ochre, carbon, and various oxides and mixtures. Although these frescos are often depicted complete, what remains of most of them are just fragments, with the remainder of the scene having been reconstructed. Most of the reconstructions were made by two Swiss painters (the Gillierons, a father and son team), on the instructions of the excavator Arthur Evans, when the fragments were found at the beginning of the 20th century. Some of these reconstructions have proved to be controversial, for example the so-called 'Prince of the Lilies', which in fact may have originally shown a priestess, and the 'Saffron Gatherers'. More details can be found under individual frescos listed.

The frescos were found mainly in **Knossos** (and associated buildings) and **Aghia Triada**, but there are also examples from **Kydonia** (Hania), Minoan villas at **Amnisos, Nirou Khani** and **Tylissos**, and a fresco from the town shrine of the island of **Pseira** (Eastern Crete).

Frescos (moving around the room in a clockwise direction):–

1 – The Blue Boy. Incorrect restoration of the Saffron Gatherers fresco (see below)

2 – Saffron Gatherer. *[Knossos, Neo-palatial]* This shows a figure gathering saffron. When the fresco was first reconstructed, Evans thought the figures were boys with black skins, but they have since been reinterpreted as blue monkeys. A similar fresco was found during the excavations of Akrotiri on the island of Santorini (Thera) where a blue monkey was depicted presenting saffron at the feet of the Goddess.

3 – The Patridge and hoopoe *[Caravanserai at Knossos, Neopalatial]*.

4 – Blue Dolphins *[Knossos, Neopalatial]*. This widely reproduced fresco was found in the so-called 'Queen's Hall' at Knossos, and a copy of it can still be seen 'in situ' there. The dolphins depicted seem to be swimming through some patterning, which has been interpreted as a net, but which in fact looks very similar to the underwater patterns of light that can still be seen today in the waters of the Meditteranean.

5 – 'La Parisienne' & 6 – Camp Stool *[Knossos, Neopalatial]*. 'La Parisienne' was so named by French workmen when they discovered the painting. This fresco depicts a high-ranking woman from Knossos, perhaps a priestess. The neckline of her garment is finished with a symbolic sacral knot, a Minoan cult symbol modelled out of a band of cloth. It was found together with 'Camp Stool' in the western block of rooms at Knossos, thought to have been a sacred area. The Camp Stool fresco shows priestesses and priests seated on stools holding chalices and goblets. Only fragements were found, so the reconstruction is not certain. 'La Parisienne' is on a larger scale than Camp Stool, which may indicate her status.

7 – Ladies in Blue. *[Knossos, Neopalatial]*. Discovered on the east wing of Knossos, the fresco depicts heads and upper torsos of three women with long tresses, headbands, and flounced dresses with open bodice. Evans suggested that the women were talking about fashion! In fact, the necklace worn by one of them is the same as that discovered in the tomb of a queen or priestess at Archanes *[see p.21]*.

8a – The Bellowing Bull *[Knossos, Neopalatial]*. This was discovered at the north entrance to Knossos, and is one of a number of frescos of bulls found at the site. The worship and veneration of bulls is thought to have been a key ritual in the religion of the Minoan civilization. The most well-known example of these frescos is:

8b – The Bull Leaper *[Knossos. Neopalatial]*. This famous fresco from the east wing depicts a ritual performed in connection with bull worship and veneration. A female is shown grasping the horns of the bull, a male vaults over the back of the animal, and a third (female) figure waits to catch him. It has been suggested that this is impossible to do, but it is still practised in the south-west of France today, though not as a sacred ritual.

9 – Griffins tethered to columns *[Great East Hall at Knossos, Neopalatial]* Griffins represent guardians of the Goddess *[see box on p.101]*.

10 – Prince of the Lilies or Priest King *[Knossos, Neopalatial]*. This famous painting, part of the 'Processional fresco', is mired in controversy. Only a few fragments from the original remained (upper body and right arm and parts of the left leg), and the reconstruction has been interpreted as a male leading an (unknown) tethered animal. However, the colour of the body was originally white, which depicts a female in Minoan art, and was only painted a light brown when reconstructed. In all other respects, the iconography also shows female attributes.

For example, the lily crown and peacock plumes depicted are usually associated with priestesses (and may have not even been attached to the figure); the necklace, which represents a collar of lilies, is similar to one found in the burial of a queen or princess at **Archanes**; and the figure is shown walking in a paradise of sacred lilies and butterflies, both symbols of the Goddess. Rodney Castleden said: "Evans made much of the Priest King, a figure he invented because of the King Minos of later legends. The Priest King fresco was Evans' best piece of evidence and that does not depict a king at all. The longest section of the Processional fresco that is susceptible of reconstruction clearly shows a female (presumably a deity) as the central focal figure. There is no sign of Evans' king".

11 – Fragments of Griffins from the wall of the Throne Room *[Knossos, Postpalatial]*.

12 – Two fragments depicting richly-dressed figures (perhaps priestesses) sitting on rocks, and mural decoration of a building, perhaps a communal shrine *[Pseira, Neopalatial]*.

13 – Procession leading a goat for sacrifice. 14 – Dancing female figurines. 15 – Procession of men. 16 – Plaster floor depicting marine landscape. *[All from Aghia Triada, Neopalatial]*.

17 – Figure of eight shields *[Knossos, Postpalatial]*. Originally found in the Hall of the Colonnades off the Grand Staircase in Knossos (now repainted 'in situ'). The markings on the shields represent the sewn animal hides from which shields were made. Rodney Castleden says of them: "Figure of eight shields are associated with the Goddess and her divine protection".

18a – Processional fresco + 18b - The Cup Bearer *[Knossos, Neopalatial]*. This fresco, which originally decorated the walls of the long ceremonial approach from the West Court to the Central Court at Knossos, originally consisted of around 536 almost life-size figures playing musical instruments and carrying vessels.

The figures are bare headed, have long wavy hair and wear tunics or long skirts. They are adorned with silver earrings, necklaces, bracelets and anklets, and some have hands raised in adoration. *[photo right]*. They make up a procession walking in from two directions. Some figures bear

jugs of liquids, and there is one particularly fine depiction of a man wearing a ceremonial skirt carrying a ritual jug called a rhyton *[photo far right]*. Standing out from the other figures is one that breaks the procession and has been interpreted as the priestess/queen of the assemblage. A group of eight adorants, four on either side, is turned towards her. The whole scene is undoubtedly a representation of an actual ceremony at Knossos involving many participants.

19 – Lily frescos *[Amnisos, Neopalatial]*. From the House of the Lilies at Amnisos.

20 – Decorations from The House of the Frescos *[Knossos, Neopalatial]* Consisting of – 20a – Riverside landscape with monkeys and aquatic plants 20b – The Blue Bird *[photo below left]*. A blue coloured bird, sitting amongst plants on a rock in a mountanous landscape. The plants include wild roses, Pancratium lilies, vetch and other flowers.
20c – Mountainous landscape with plants and a blue monkey *[photo below right]*.

This concludes the frescos on display in this gallery. From here an open door leads to the rest of the Museum, moving in an anti-clockwise direction.

From Gallery 2 through corridor:
Metaxis Collection
Gimalkis Collection
Private collections of antiquities donated to the Museum at various times.

The following galleries all date from later periods, and are of interest chiefly for the occasional examples that they show of the survival of a Goddess culture into later times.
Gallery: Classical, Hellenistic, Roman [Cemeteries] 5th-4th century BCE
Corridor – Cretan coinage
Gallery: Classical, Hellenistic, Roman [Cities & Sanctuaries] 5th-4thC BCE
includes – the Sanctuary of Demeter at Knossos, and the Sanctuary of Demeter and Kore at **Gortyn**.
Gallery: Geometric, Archaic, Classical 10th-4th century BCE
includes – a figure standing between two water birds, representing the Minoan nature Goddess, in a version recalling her ephiphany between birds *[see box on p.18]*. Her vegetation and fertility aspects are stressed by a model of trees that she holds in her hand.
Gallery: Cemetery of the city state of Rezinia & other sites
includes – from a tomb at Phythies (Archanes area) from the Geometric period (late 9thC BCE), a shrine model containing the figure of a Goddess with upraised arms. Two prone male figures, perhaps worshippers, and an animal observe the Goddess through an opening in the roof. This probably echoes beliefs about the forms of contact between the terrestrial world and the underworld and ways of invoking the goddess-protectress of the deceased.

Model of shrine with Goddess inside

Gallery: Geometric, Archaic, Classical [Sanctuaries] 10th-4th century BCE
includes (1) – figurine of a naked man walking and holding a wreath representing ritual offerings. Similar offerings were made at sanctuaries of Cretan ferility goddesses, such as Diktynna, Eileithyia, Europa Elotia and Ariadne.
(2) – large clay female figure with helmet, representing Athena Promachos, from the sanctuary at **Gortyn** [Archaic, 7th century BCE]
(3) – finds from the Sanctuary of Hermes and Aphrodite at **Kato Symi**, the Sanctuary of Athena at **Smari**, and the Sanctuary of Athena on the Acropolis of **Gortyn** [all Archaic 8th-7th centuries BCE]
(4) – finds from the **Idean Cave** (jug and double axes) and the **Dicktean** cave.

Gallery: Geometric, Archaic, Classical [Sanctuaries] 10th-4th century BCE (cont).

(5) – finds from the cave of Eileithyia (Goddess of protection in childbirth) at **Inatos**, covering the Protopalatial to the Roman period (4th century CE), with a peak from the late 11th to early 6th centuries BCE. These include figurines of couples and pregnant women, double axes *[see box on p.14]*, and two female equestrian riders. These are first attested in the Postpalatial (Mycenean) period (13th-12th centuries BCE) and became widespread during early historic times, but only a few examples have been found in Crete. They are believed to depict a nature Goddess with fertility attributes, such as Artemis or Eileithyia. This particular find *[photo right]* was from **Archanes** in the Geometric period (10th-mid 9th century BCE).

Riders depicting nature Goddesses

(6) – a terracotta plaque depicting in relief a female with upraised arms (survival of GUA motif). From Mathia, Pediada area, Archaic (7th century BCE).

Corridor: trade and cultural influences with Egypt, Cyprus, Attica, etc.

Gallery: Geometric, Archaic, Classical [Cities and Settlements] 10th-4th centuries BCE. Includes – finds from **Praisos** (Eteo Cretan centre), including clay and votive material, including clay figurines.

Corridor & Gallery: Iron Age

This concludes the tour of the Heraklion Museum

AFTER THE MINOANS. Although the Minoan civilisation and culture may have declined in the Postpalatial and later periods (from 1100 BCE onwards), the love and celebration of a Goddess or Goddesses did not disappear overnight. Some Minoan people retreated to inaccessible mountain refuge sites, where they attempted to continue with their old customs and beliefs. But, perhaps more significantly, the remnants of the Minoan (and later Mycenean) people formed the nucleus of the emerging Greek (EteoCretan) city-state society, whose beliefs were polytheistic, and later included worship of named Goddesses familiar to us today, such as Demeter, Artemis (or Britomartis or Dicktynna as she was often called in Crete), Hera, Athena, Ariadne, Aphrodite, etc. These later cultures from the Geometric, Archaic and Hellenistic periods still seemed to have retained a belief in Goddess(es), though the magnificent days of Minoan culture were a memory.

KNOSSOS

Open: April-mid Oct, Daily 0800-2000. Mid Oct-Apr: Mon-Fri 0800-1500, Sat & Sun 08.30-1500.
Location: 6km south of Heraklion – signposted from City Centre and from the National Road. Busses run frequently, and many coach tours go there.

Summary: Knossos is a 'must see' site, the finest temple-palace on Crete, and, because of the reconstructions of Sir Arthur Evans (made in the early years of the 20th century), one that has a sense of how it must have originally looked. However there are some downsides: some of the reconstructions are controversial, particularly the names and attributions of some of the rooms that Evans made; the site wardens are very strict and will readily shout and blow whistles if you stray off the main paths; and the site is very often heaving with coach parties and tour guides. There are 'official' tour guides that will take you round (for a fee), but beware that their interpretations and information are often out-of-date and inappropriate for anyone who does not want to be fed the 'King Minos' orthodoxy.

Reconstruction of how Knossos probably looked
at the height of the Neopalatial period

History of Knossos

Neolithic. There was a Neolithic village on a low hill known as Kephali in the valley of the Kairatos river as early as 7000 BCE. The settlers built simple rectangular mud-brick buildings on stone foundations. They practised mixed farming, and later developed the ability to produce fired pots. By the Late Neolithic the settlement covered five hectares.

Prepalatial period. From 3500 BCE onwards the Prepalatial settlement expanded and buildings became more substantial. There was contact and trade with the outside world, and by the end of this period traces of a monumental building were discovered in the north-west area of the settlement (near to the later Throne Room), which may have been a predecessor to the first Palace-Temple.

Protopalatial period (Old Palace). The first Palace-Temple was built soon after 1900 BCE. Extensive deposits of pottery were found beneath the first major building, which was placed over a number of earlier houses. The building itself originally consisted of a number of separate units, which over time were joined together. The original Palace-Temple included the Central Court, with rooms on the west side opening onto it. Outside the site, a West Court was also constructed. Storage rooms were constructed on both the west and east sides, which involved some remodelling of the Kephali hill on the east side. Cemetries from this period have been found across the river and on the Gypsades hill to the south.

Neopalatial period (New Palace) A great fire destroyed the first Palace-Temple around 1700 BCE, but it was rebuilt straight away. An earthquake then destroyed part of it but it was rebuilt, along with other neighbouring houses and villas (such as the Treasury, House of the Frescos, South House, House of the Chancel Screen, Little Palace, Royal Villa and Temple Tomb). This period represents the finest flowering of Minoan culture. The frescos were painted; the Throne Room and Central Shrine area constructed; the figurines (such as the 'Snake Goddesses' Bull Leaper and Lionesse's Head rhyton) and seal rings created; and the rooms and walkways extended so that the site eventually covered over 20,000 sq metres.

Postpalatial period. At the end of the Neopalatial period (around 1450 BCE) a great conflagration swept through Crete, but while most sites were abandoned at this time, the damage at Knossos seems to have been less. The Palace-Temple continued in use, though it is likely to have been occupied by Myceneans from the Mainland, who brought with them new burial customs. However, they continued to be Goddess-celebrating, although the style of the figurines changed. The room known as 'The Shrine of the Double Axes' was brought into use, and remains of Goddesses with Upraised Arms *[see p.23]* from this period were found there. Tablets inscribed with Linear B script *[see p.12]* also date from this period. However, the centre of power in Crete was changing, and eventually moved to Kydonia in the west (modern day Hania), although Knossos remained significant.

Plan of Knossos

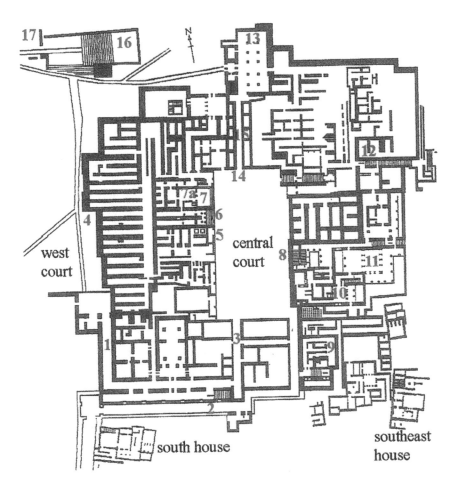

1. *Corridor of the Procession*
2. *Horns of Consecration*
3. *'Prince of Lilies' fresco*
4. *West magazines*
5. *Temple repositories & pillar crypts*
6. *Steps to upper floor*
7. *Throne room*
7a. *Central shrine area*
8. *Grand staircase*
9. *Shrine of the Double Axes*
10. *'Queens Hall'*
11. *Hall of the Double Axes*
12. *Giant Pithoi*
13. *North pillar hall*
14. *North entrance corridor*
15. *Charging bull fresco*
16. *Theatral area*
17. *Royal road*

Tour of Knossos

Knossos originally consisted of buildings of at least two storeys, but what is seen today is generally the lower storey. You enter the site on the western side, and walk past three large pits called **Kouloures**, which may have originally contained grain, but by the end of the Protopalatial (Old Palace) period were filled with rubbish, including much broken pottery of high quality, and then paved over. Immediately next to them are the remains of the **West Court**, which extends to the west facade of the site. Behind it there is a recess which would formerly have held a window in the storey above. It has been suggested that these windows were used for ceremonial appearances by the Priestesses of Knossos.

You now enter the **Corridor of the Procession** (1), which at its entrance were found traces of frescos of bulls' hooves. Entry was effected through huge wooden doors, so that entering the site must have seemed like entry into a sacred world. Frescos adorned the walls of the Corridor, depicting figures playing musical instruments and carrying vessels *[see p.29-30]*. Part of one of these frescos 'The Cup Bearer' has been reconstructed on site. The Corridor turns sharp left and in the centre of it are giant **Horns of Consecration** (2) *[see p.15]*, over 2 metres high. These have been reconstructed from fragments found during excavation, and would originally have adorned the south front of the building. They are beautifully aligned to the distant horned peak of **Mount Juktas**, a sacred mountain to the Minoan people (though vegetation growth has nowadays all but obscured the view).

SACRED MOUNTAINS. The Minoan people had a great love, awe and respect for mountains and high places, which they may have thought were the abode of the Goddess. It was on mountains that they constructed their Peak Sanctuaries *[see box on p.16]*, and many of their Palace-Temple sites and other buildings were oriented to neighbouring mountain peaks. A number of these have distinctive horned shapes, so it is easy to see why these horns were then replicated in the buildings that faced them. **Mt. Jucktas** is a good example, being both a horned peak and a Peak Sanctuary, and a miniature painting found at Knossos *[see p.15]* may be an illustration of the shrine on Mt.Jucktas itself. At **Vasiliki**, the site also seems to be aligned on a distant horned mountain, and at **Phaistos** the Temple-Palace site is aligned on a similar sacred mountain of **Mt. Ida**.

The Corridor of the Procession now turns sharp left again to lead into the **Central Court**, on the south side of which is Evans' controversial reconstruction of the 'Prince of Lilies' fresco *[see p.29]*. The Central Court is oriented NNE-SSW, a feature it shares in common with the other Palace-Temple sites of Phaistos, Malia and Zakros. It has been suggested that the Central Court was used for public spectacles, including ceremonies and bull-leaping activities. All the Central Courts have shrines on the west wings and ceremonial areas on the east wings.

Turning to the west wing, there are two parallel lines of rooms. The further line of rooms are called the **West Magazines** (4), and consisted of 18 storerooms containing pithoi (large jars) which held grain, oil and wine. Pyramidial stone stands were found in the corridor, which originally would have held double axes on poles *[see p.14]*.

The nearer line of rooms (next to the Central Court) consisted of the sacred heart of the site. **The Temple Repositories and Pillar Crypts** (5) *[see box below]* were adjoining rooms, shielded by a Tripartite Shrine, which consisted of pairs of columns flanked by a block supporting a single column, all crowned with horns of consecration. This would have been a magnificent indication of the sacred nature of the rooms behind. The **Temple Repositories** had two large stone containers sunk under the floor, which held several figurines, including the two Snake Priestesses *[see p.19]* together with shells, gold foil, fragments of worked ivory, rock crystal, bronze and stone implements, clay sealings, inlays and plaques.

PILLAR CRYPTS. These were enclosed rooms without natural light, each with a central pillar. They were dark and mysterious, and doubtless connected with preparations to be made for ceremonies and rituals. At **Knossos** the east Pillar Crypt (above) had 13 double axe carvings on the central pillar, and the west Pillar Crypt (above) had 17 on its central pillar, indicating their ritual significance. There were troughs on the floors beside the pillars which may have received liquid offerings. Finds include storage jars, burnt offerings, cups and pottery sherds. Nanno Marinatos has suggested that the rites celebrated in the crypts were concerned with grain production and the cycle of the seasons, and Marina Moss has also suggested that it was a Goddess of renewal who was celebrated in there.

We now come to the very heart of this ceremonial area - the **Throne Room** (7) and the **Central Shrine Area** (7a). These two rooms adjoined each other, and the Central Shrine area may have been the room where the Priestess waited before entering the Throne Room for the purpose of enacting a powerful ritual.

In the Central Shrine area Evans found Postpalatial seal impressions, including one showing an Artemis-like "Mountain Mother" or "Lady of the Beasts". She is shown standing on a mountain (perhaps a Peak Sanctuary – *see p.16*), flanked by two lionesses. Behind her is an altar surmounted by horns of consecration, and in front of her a male worshipper salutes her, a characteristic pose of male adorants of the Goddess (also found in many small  figurines given as votive offerings). Seal rings like this were undoubtedly worn by Priestesses, and the discovery of this one in the Central Shrine room shows that this sacred area continued in use in the Postpalatial period.

Although none of these inner rooms, the Temple Repositories, Pillar Crypts or Central Shrine are now visible or accessible to the public today, the **Throne Room** may be viewed through a window from the Central Court. This room was in use in the Protopalatial period, continued throughout the Neopalatial period, and was remodelled in the Postpalatial period. It contains an alabaster throne, gypsum benches, a large bowl and restored frescoes of guardian griffins *[see box on p.101]* and may originally have portrayed scenes from the natural world. Steps from the room lead down to a lustral basin.

LUSTRAL BASINS, also known as Adyton, are a feature of all the Palace-Temple sites and some villas, and some 25 or so examples have been found. They usually take the form of a small sunken rectangular room, often entered by a staircase. It is thought that they were used for ritual cleansing and purification, and religious objects and iconography have sometimes been found in them. People probably purified themselves by means of sanctified water, either by bathing or sprinkling before taking part in religious ceremonies. It has been suggested that Lustral Basins were originally created as imitations of sacred caves *[see p.63]*.

Evans suggested that the Throne Room was a meeting place, presided over by his fictitious King Minos, but it is generally accepted nowadays that it was the location for an epiphany ritual, with a priestess appearing robed from the Central Shrine room to sit on the throne and embody the Minoan Goddess. This must have been an incredibly powerful experience, perhaps witnessed by selected people, who would view it from their bench seats inside the Throne Room itself.

Recently, Lucy Goodison has suggested that the Throne Room and adjoining rooms may have been used to create dramatic lighting effects at sunrise at certain times of the year, whereby the rising sun would shine through specific doorways to illuminate particular areas that would have been used for ritual purposes. Goodison gained entry to the Throne Room and adjoining rooms at particular times and observed how this might have occured. She discovered that dawn light entering through one of the Anteroom doors (extreme right) at *midwinter sunrise* reached right into the Throne Room itself, a normally unlit interior space, where it would have illuminated the figure of a Priestess on the 'throne'. Close to the

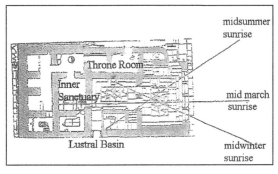

equinoxes it would have entered another door (second from right) to illuminate the Inner Sanctuary, which Evans felt was the location for "a vision of the Goddess herself and her divine associates". At the "times of the dead" *(early September)* the light would have entered through the next door along (second from left); and finally, at the *midsummer sunrise* it would have entered through the door on the extreme left to illuminate the Lustral Basin.

If this is what happened, then we may picture, for example, the dramatic scene of the Epiphany of the Goddess, embodied by a Priestess on the throne in the Throne Room as occuring at the winter solstice, the shortest day of the year before the rebirth of the sun. It is known that at Knossos, rooms and suites of rooms were divided by folding doors that could be opened and closed. Perhaps the Anteroom doors were closed for the ritual, which took place by torchlight, and at the moment of the epiphany they would be dramatically pushed open and the rising sun would shine on the embodied priestess, as the Goddess descended into her. This would be seen by the spectators as being the living presence of the Goddess from the sun.

Moving across the **Central Court** (oriented NNE-SSW) to the eastern suite of rooms, there is the reconstructed **Grand Staircase** (8), with two double flights of broad steps, made from gypsum (a crystalline form of alabaster). These originally led to a large room that Evans dubbed The Great East Hall, though Rodney Castleden argues that it should more properly be called 'The Sanctuary of the Great Goddess'. The room was decorated with frescos, and there was a collection of miniature sanctuary equipment. Bronze fittings for a large wooden statue of a Goddess were found, which would have been about 3 metres high. Nothing now remains of this statue and the room has been destroyed.

The rest of this eastern side of the site appears to consist mainly of domestic and store rooms, though some of the names Evans attributed to them (e.g The Queen's Toilet and Bath) are, to say the least, fanciful. The so-called '**Queen's Hall**' (10) consists of reconstructions of some of the frescos found 'in situ' (though probably fallen from what may have been a shrine in a room above), such as the Blue Dolphins *[see p.27]*, and a panel featuring 'dancing girls', showing a female with hair rising above her head. In fact this is not a 'dancing girl' but is the characteristic depiction of a descending Goddess in an epiphany scene *[see box on p.18]*. The room and these reconstructed frescos may be viewed through windows.

Two rooms on this eastern side that are worthy of note are the **Shrine of the Double Axes** (9) and **Hall of the Double Axes** (11). These two rooms are very different and date from different periods. The **Shrine of the Double Axes** (9) is a small room, dating from the Final Palace period at Knossos *[see p.21]*. The room consisted of three different floor levels, with a shallow anteroom in front. On the foremost level, there were a number of vases probably used to contain offerings. The central level supported a round tripod altar or table of offerings. At the back there was a ledge, on which stood several ritual objects, including two pairs of horns of consecration, with small sockets, possibly for the insertion of double axes *[see box on p.14]*, a small stealite double axe, and a number of figurines representing Goddesses and votaries or priestesses. One of the best finds was of a Goddess with Upraised Arms (GUA), wearing necklaces and bracelets, a seal on each wrist, and a dove perching on her head, now in Heraklion Museum *[photo right and see p.22-23]*. This room shows that Goddess worship continued after the destruction of the site by the 1450BCE conflagration.

Immediately north of this Shrine room was another small room that had a similar shelf-like ledge, that may also have held Goddess figurines. In this room was found a triton shell, that Evans suggested was used to call in the deity. North of the Shrine of the Double Axes and the Triton Shell room, there is the 'Queens Hall', and north of this lies the room called by Evans **The Hall of the Double Axes** (11). This consisted of two underground interconnected sanctuary suites, one large outer one and one small inner one, together with a stairwell. Against the wall of the outer chamber, Evans found the remains of a canopied throne. Castleden comments that we do not know whether a life-sized statue of a deity sat there, or a priestess conducting a ritual, or a priestess as the epiphany of the Goddess. In the inner room, 'masons marks' were depicted, giving the room its name. Going into these dark rooms would have felt like descending into the underworld, a place well fitted to carry out chthonic rituals.

Moving further northwards, among the rooms of interest are the one housing **giant pithoi** (12), and the **North Pillar Hall** (13) that has a double row of gypsum pillars which are thought to have supported a dining hall above, and the **North Entrance Corridor** (14), with 'masons marks' of tridents and double axes. This corridor is dominated by a copy of a large reconstructed fresco **The Bellowing Bull** (15) *[see p.28 (8a)]*. It has been suggested that this fresco, which was probably still standing in later Greek times, must have lent some colour to the legend of the Minatour.

THE LABYRINTH AND THE MINATOUR. The legend of the labyrinth of Crete that housed the monstrous creature, the minatour, is very well known. The legend is linked to Knossos, although no labyrinth has ever been found there. (However, Rodney Castleden has suggested that the whole site itself is a carefully designed labyrinth). The legend tells of how King Minos' wife Queen Pasiphae (the daughter of Helios, the sun god, and probably a moon goddess in her own right) was made by Poseidon (god of the sea) to fall in love with the bull Asterios. From their union came the half-man half-bull creature the minatour, to whom every year seven men and seven women from Athens were sacrificed. Determined to stop this, Theseus, prince of Athens, came to Crete to slay the bull. He was aided in his journey through the labyrinth by Ariadne, daughter of King Minos, and after slaying the bull, the two lovers escaped to the island of Naxos, where Theseus abandoned her. This mythic tale would appear to have no historical verification, except that curiously one of the Linear B tablets found at Knossos mentions 'Our Lady of the Labyrinth'. So, with both the bull cult and some kind of labyrinth ceremony at Knossos, there may be some foundation to the myth.

At this NORTH entrance to the site, there was a **Theatral Area** (16), perhaps designed for some performance or spectacle. From here a well-paved road, the **Royal Road** (17) originally led westwards into the Minoan town of Knossos. It was lined with buildings, including the building named by Evans **The House of Frescos**. From here came the blue bird scene, and one with blue monkeys *[see p.30 frescos no.20 a-c]*. Further on, the road led towards **The Little Palace**. This was an elaborate building, with a paved peristyle court, a stately main hall and a number of rooms. West of the hall there was originally a lustral basin *[see box on p.38]* converted into a shrine that contained a pair of horns of consecration *[see box on p.15]* and four curious natural stalagmite formations vaguely resembling human forms. In the southern part of the building there were a suite of pillar crypts *[see box on p.37]*, where a collection of religious objects were found, having fallen from the floor above. These included a double-axe stand, a lead figurine of the Snake Priestess *[see p.19]* and a magnificent bull's head rhyton *[illustrated on p.20]*. Behind the Little Palace lay a large Minoan building named by Evans **The Unexplored Mansion**, as he uncovered only its eastern facade, though excavation has now been completed. It was joined to the Little Palace by a bridge and divided into three sections. It burned down in the Postpalatial period, but part of it was re-occupied in later times. West of this is the **North House (House of the Children's Bones)** where remains of four children were found in 1959. It was suggested that this was a human sacrifice, but recently this theory has been questioned, and been instead attributed to a secondary burial *[see box on p.47]*.

Returning to the Palace-Temple site itself, and moving to the SOUTH of the site, there are five buildings within the perimeter of the Palace-Temple site that are of interest. Firstly, there is the **South East House**, an elegant Neopalatial building. On its north side there was a pillar crypt *[see box on p.37]* with two double-axe stands and a niche that may have been for offerings. Next to this there is the poorly preserved **House of the Chancel Screen**, to the west of which are the remains of the **House of the Fallen Blocks**, that was toppled by an earthquake in approx. 1700 BCE. Next to this is the basement of another building felled at the same time, called by Evans **House of the Sacrificed Oxen**, from two heads of sacrificed oxen in front of the altars. This may have occured at the time of the earthquake, as an attempt to ward off further destruction. Finally, further west there is the **South House**, which stood beside the Minoan road on the southern approach to the Palace-Temple site. It is partially restored on three levels, and contains features familiar from other buildings, including a lustral basin *[see box on p.38]*, a room with a central pillar and stand for a double axe, and pillar crypts *[see box on p.37]* in the basement. Silver vessels and a hoard of bronze tools were found in the remains.

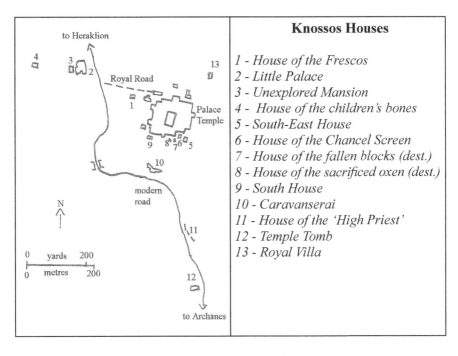

	Knossos Houses
to Heraklion	
	1 - House of the Frescos
Royal Road	*2 - Little Palace*
	3 - Unexplored Mansion
Palace Temple	*4 - House of the children's bones*
	5 - South-East House
	6 - House of the Chancel Screen
	7 - House of the fallen blocks (dest.)
	8 - House of the sacrificed oxen (dest.)
modern road	*9 - South House*
N	*10 - Caravanserai*
	11 - House of the 'High Priest'
0 yards 200	*12 - Temple Tomb*
0 metres 200	*13 - Royal Villa*
to Archanes	

Moving further south along the old Minoan road, are the remains of buildings called by Evans the **Caravanserai**, as he believed that travellers would stop there to rest before entering the Palace-Temple site. It had two main rooms approached by stepped passages, and a spring and large public stone bath for washing feet. Nearby was a small underground spring chamber, where finds were made of offertory vessels and a clay model of a little round hut-shaped urn containing a figurine of a Goddess with Upraised Arms. There was also on the walls a fresco showing a natural scene of a partridge and hoopoes, which is now in the frescos room at Heraklion Mueum *[see p.27]*. The next important building southwards is the one called by Evans **The House of the High Priest**, so-named from a stone altar found there, flanked by stands for double axes. If it was the house of an officiant at the main site, then it is much more likely to have been a priestess rather than a priest. South of this lay the building named the **Temple Tomb**. This building was on a grand scale, with the entrance resembling a tripartite shrine. Inside, steps descended into the darkness of a pillar crypt *[see box on p.37]*, with two massive pillars and walls inscribed with a double axe carving. An ossary contained the bones of 20 bodies, and there was also a funerary chamber, whose original ceiling was painted a deep blue as if to imitate the sky. Finally, to the NE of the main site, the **Royal Villa** had a central hall (where a throne was found and a pillar crypt) and upper floor. Clearly it was an important site for ritual and ceremony.

SOUTH OF KNOSSOS

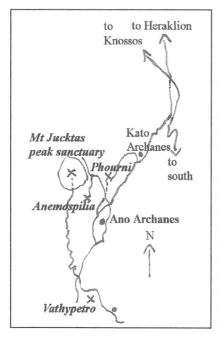

Follow the road south from **Knossos** (or drive direct from Heraklion), and at a roundabout, take the road for **Archanes**. There is a cluster of Minoan sites here, two of which (**Phourni** and **Mt. Jucktas**) would have been the destination for pilgrimages, either to carry the dead and/or to make offerings at the peak sanctuary. There is also the temple of **Anemospilia**, which may tell the story of a very unusual human sacrifice made at the end of the Protopalatial period, and finally the villa at **Vathypetro**, set in idyllic surroundings amongst the hills. The road from Knossos reaches Kato (Lower) Archanes, from where a sharp right turn winds its way up to **Phourni** cemetery. The site can also be reached on foot from the town of Ano (Upper) Archanes (signposted).

PHOURNI

Phourni is Crete's richest and most significant burial site, a high status site with rich finds. It was in use throughout the whole Minoan period of over 1000 years, from Prepalatial to Postpalatial times, with individual tombs in use for hundreds of years and others added later. It consists of two tomb types: tholos tombs (characteristic of those from the **Mesara Plain** *[see box on p.71]*), and house tombs, typical of those in central and east Crete. There is evidence of the two cultural elements being combined here in one place. 24 funerary buildings of different kinds have been uncovered from various periods, including house tombs, tholos tombs, tholos tomb ante-chambers, Mycenean shaft graves, burial mounds and a libation pit. Rich grave goods were discovered, including a Goddess libation vessel, figurines of birds and animals, necklaces, a bronze mirror, gold rings, bronze daggers, seal stones, Cycladic-style Goddess figurines and pottery – a real cornucopia of offerings. It seems probable that there was a permanent presence of priestesses here who looked after the tombs, attended to the dead bodies and presided over a 'cult of the dead' *[see box on p.47]*.

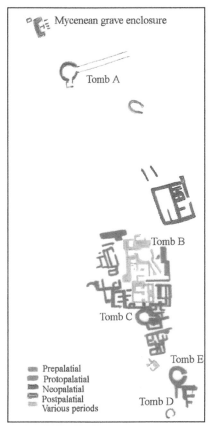

Mycenean grave enclosure

Tomb A

Tomb B

Tomb C

Tomb E

Tomb D

Prepalatial
Protopalatial
Neopalatial
Postpalatial
Various periods

Tholos tomb E with Mt.Jucktas behind

The earliest tomb is probably **Tholos E**, which dates from the early Prepalatial period EMII [2400-2300 BCE]. It was built above ground, and contained a large number of burials, with 117 offerings found (including 8 sealstones). The burials were subsequently destroyed when the tomb was re-used 200 years later, in the late Prepalatial period [MMIA], which produced evidence of 56 burials, of which 36 were contained in 29 larnakes and 2 pithoi, while other burials had been placed on the ground between the larnakes. Once again there were funerary offerings including sealstones.

Another tomb dating back to the Prepalatial period [EMIII - 2250-2100 BCE] was **Tholos C**, again built above ground. It was known to be vaulted, and had a funerary building butressed onto the eastern and southern side. 11 larnakes were found in the tomb, together with a pithos burial, containing the remains of 18 people in total. 24 bodies had been buried between the larnakes and 3 more in the entrance, giving a total of 45. A rich assortment of artefacts had been carefully deposited as funerary offerings, including 80 sea shells, 11 ivory seals, 3 bronze daggers, precious jewellery, and fragments of 15 Cycladic Goddess figurines, made of marble, schist, quartz and ivory *[see box on p.104]*. The tomb was in use for many years.

South and east of Tholos tomb C are the remains of a funerary building, dating back to the end of the Prepalatial period. Offerings found here included miniature bull figurines, two bull rhytons, and a clay model of a sistrum. There were 172 infant and child burials in this funerary building.

The other tomb begun in the Prepalatial period [MMIA – before 2000 BCE] was **Tholos B**, which was probably built over an important funerary area from an earlier time. The tholos tomb was reached by a dromos (passageway) from the SE side, and the tholos had two side chambers. The tholos tomb was set amongst funerary buildings, which eventually became a large rectangular complex of two storeys. Amongst the buildings were a south-west chamber, built around a larnax which was an ossary containing the bones of 19 people, including 2 children.

A room to the south was added, which was a pillar crypt *[see box on p.37]*, which abutted what was then the outer wall of the tholos. Above it was a crypt, which remained in use for a long period, and has yielded a silver pin with Linear A inscription *[see box on p.12]* and a gold ring depicting a goddess and a griffin *[see box on p.101]*. This complex of funerary buildings remained in use for more than 600 years right up until the Postpalatial period.

Pillar crypt at Tholos B complex

The remaining 2 tholoses both date from the later Postpalatial period [LMIIIA]. **Tholos A** came into use around the time of the destruction of **Knossos**, indicating that this site of Phourni continued into use after the fall of the Minoan culture. It has a long east-facing dromos, and is one of the best preserved tombs of its type, being still roofed, and with a small rock-cut side chamber. There was a single burial in a sealed larnax of what was obviously a high-ranking female, probably a member of the royal family or a priestess. Buried with her were 140 pieces of gold jewellery *[see p.21]*. On the floor of the side chamber next to the larnax were 10 bronze vessels and 87 pieces of ivory inlay that had decorated a wooden

Tholos tomb A

footstool. There was also the remains of a horse sacrifice and the skull of a bull. North of this tholos were found the remains of **Mycenean Graves**, also dating from the Postpalatial period. Seven shaft graves have survived, each of which contained a larnax with painted decoration, but which were broken and empty. Many rich grave offerings remained in the graves, which suggested that the bodies were ritually exhumed for secondary burial in the same Postpalatial period.

Finally, **Tholos D** at the southern end of the site, also dates from the Postpalatial period, and, like Tholos A, also contained only one burial, once again a wealthy female probably from the Royal Family. She was found with a bronze mirror in her hand in front of her face, and on her head she wore a single gold diadem, while 3 necklaces adorned her breast. The first of these consisted of 50 beads: 20 granular and globular beads made of gold, 29 made of glass paste and one of sard. The second was made up of 32 faience beads, and the third of 15 drop-like beads, also of faience. Two gold rings were found, which would have held her hair, and she had been wearing a garment that was made of 67 gold beads with twelve-petal rosettes. Other items of gold and faience were placed in the tomb with her.

Together these two extremely rich and lavish burials in Tholoses A & D show that the internments in these tombs had changed from the group and communal burials of the Prepalatial and Protopalatial periods to much more individual and wealthy burials in the Postpalatial period. This burial in Tholos D really marks the end of the use of Phourni cemetary, and after this the site became abandoned.

CULT OF THE DEAD. The Cult arose in Prepalatial Crete and continued in some cemeteries, notably **Phourni**, well into the Palatial period. It is regarded as the earliest example of communal ritual practice in Minoan Crete. The most impressive and monumental structures created at this time were the tombs, which varied in size and style depending on regional taste. **Mochlos** had rock cut tombs, whilst the **Mesara** plains had free-standing dome-shaped tholoses *[see box on p.71]*. Despite architectural differences, both have evidence of an existing 'Cult of the Dead'. The cult had priestesses/priests who usually lived on site to oversee activities and the production of goods (for example, wine and olive oil) which would have been used in ceremonies. They would officiate at simple or family burials, which took place shortly following death (personal possessions accompanied the deceased), and also at more elaborate public funerary rites and ritual activities, as well as toasting ceremonies and festivals which honoured the dead or the seasons. Secondary burials would take place once the corpse had become a skeleton. A chosen principal bone, either thigh or skull, would be removed from the tomb and placed into the communal ossuary. No longer an individual, this person became a communal ancestor. It was the responsibility of the priestesses/priests to handle and securely store any cultic equipment, such as the Goddess libation vessels, used during ritual activity. The Cult of the Dead did not cease at the onset of the Palatial era, but transformed and diversified. Communal cults now took place at Peak Sanctuaries *[see box on p.16]* and within sacred caves *[see box on p.63]*, whilst within the Temple-Palaces the Pillar Crypts *[see box on p.37]* were used.

ARCHANES

Continuing down the main road, there is the town of Ano (Upper) Archanes, built over an original Minoan Palace-Temple type site at the beginning of the Protopalatial period (around 1900 BCE), which continued to be occupied until the end of the Neopalatial period in 1450 BCE, when the site was destroyed by the great conflagration. (There is some evidence for limited re-occupation in the Postpalatial period). This was an extensive and elaborate site that, due to the existence of modern buildings, has been difficult to excavate, though part of the excavation can be seen in the Tourkogeitonia part of the town (off a street parallel to the main street, near to a reservoir). Here was found evidence of substantial Minoan buildings of a scale similar to those of **Knossos**, **Malia**, **Phaistos** and **Zakros**. Remains of living quarters, courtyards, wall frescos (one depicting a priestess holding a branch), altars and shrines point up the links to other Palace-Temple sites. Finds included pottery of the marine style, anthropormorphic and other figurines (including some made of ivory finished with gold leaf), several horns of consecration *[see box on p.15]*, loom weights and whorls, decorated clay vases (one of which contained a triton shell), stone lamps and ritual jars. All this points to an extensive ceremonial and ritual site with associated workshops, storage rooms and living quarters. It was suggested by Evans and the late 20th century excavators of the site, J & E Sakellarakis, that the procession made to the Peak Sanctuary of **Mt. Jucktas** began from Archanes.

There is a small Archaeological Museum in Archanes, which has information on the site and finds at Archanes and Phourni. (Open daily except Mondays).

ANEMOSPILIA

The Minoan temple site of Anemospilia lies in the foothills of **Mt. Jucktas**, about 3km north-west of Archanes. Take a turning west of the main road and follow the road as it winds upwards to the site, which lies to the left of this minor road. This is a unique site in Minoan architecture, consisting of three rectangular rooms, with a long corridor to the north of them. The excavators of

the site (J & E Sakellarakis) interpreted it as a temple or shrine, due to the large quantities of ritual artefacts that were discovered, including ritual vases, a chalice, pithoi, a rhyton, etc, and suggested that it might be a kind of tripartite shrine, similar to those built on Peak Sanctuaries *[see p.16]*. The site was in use during the Protopalatial period.

The site was discovered in 1979, and it has become notorious as virtually the only example of human sacrifice in the whole of Minoan society, though this interpretation has recently been challenged. The excavators suggested that the three rooms had different functions. They thought that the eastern room was the venue for 'bloodless' ritual ceremonies. There was a stepped altar in the room, on the top of which were ritual vessels and utensils, one of which had a Linear A inscription *[see box on p.12]*. The excavators compare it to a scene on the **Aghia Triada** sarcophagus *[see p.24-5]*, which depicts offerings of fruits being made to the Earth Mother. They paint a picture of a scene where fruit, crops and vegetables, together with liquids such as wine and oil, and aromatic herbs, are made as offerings to a Goddess of Nature.

The **central room** was packed with the shrine's larger vessels and utensils. Apart from pithoi found along the length of the walls, the entire floor was covered with vases, with the exception of two sections, where a bench had been placed. It was here that a very unusual object was found: a pair of very large clay feet *[photo right]* which the excavators thought had belonged to a large wooden statue of a goddess that had stood on the bench.

The **western room** is the one where the supposed human sacrifice had taken place. The excavators found three human skeletons (with a fourth in the process of fleeing from the central room). One of these was a young man of about 18, who lay on an altar, together with a long bronze knife. His legs seem to have been bound, and an examination of his bones revealed that his body had been drained of blood. The two other skeletons in the room were of a high-status woman and man, interpreted as the high priestess and priest carrying out the sacrifice. Moments later, an earthquake had struck the site (around 1700 BCE), killing all the living participants, including the one fleeing out of the site. If true, this was certainly a dramatic occurrence, and J & E Sakellarakiss point out that as human sacrifice was not otherwise known in this peaceful Minoan society, this must have happened at a time of real desperation, perhaps because of repeated earthquake activity. However, this interpretation of sacrifice has been recently challenged by Dennis Hughes, who finds other, less sinister, explanations for the knife (could be a ritual spear), the 'altar' (which was different to usual altars), the supposed binding of the legs (could have been caused by the temple falling in) and the lack of blood (could have been caused by the fire burning after the earthquake). Whatever the truth, this is a most intriguing site.

Mt. JUCKTAS

Mt. Jucktas can be reached by taking an unmade road signposted off the main road to the south of **Archanes**. Drive or walk to the top, and just before the church, take a paved path on the right to the Peak Sanctuary. This was perhaps the most important Peak Sanctuary in Minoan times *[see box on p.16]*, a place of pilgrimage for more than 1000 years. It was visible from **Knossos** *[see p.36]* from where journeys to it would have commenced, and also from **Archanes**, which may have had a special relationship with it.

At the Peak Sanctuary, there are two terraces with the remains of buildings and a rectangular enclosure, which were designed for ritual practices. A stepped altar was constructed, and next to it was a large stone kernos (offering stone) with around 100 circular depressions *[see box on p.57]*. A hoard of bronze double axes *[see box on p.14]* were found, together with vessels for libation and offering tables. At the centre of this Peak Sanctuary is a natural chasm 10m deep, into which offerings were thrown. Hundreds of terracotta figurines, both animal and human (including heads and

Top – Mt.Jucktas. Middle – Peak Sanctuary at summit. Bottom – Chasm where ritual offerings were thrown

limbs) were recovered from the cleft, showing that apotropaic offerings to the Goddess had been made over a long period of time. A fragment of a Postpalatial [LMIIIC] GUA *[see box on p.23]* was also found. Nearby on the surface, evidence for workshops and a potter's kiln (from the Neopalatial period) were discovered, showing that some of the objects offered may have been made on site.

On the south-west slope of the mountain at 400m there is a cave, Stravomyti, which consists of a network of raised natural passageways and larger areas, one with an enclosed pond. This cave was used in Neolithic times for burial and refuge, and continued into Minoan times as a sacred cave *[see box on p.63]*.

VATHYPETRO

Returning to the main road and travelling further south, we reach Vathypetro, a large country villa, built in the Neopalatial [LMI] period, probably for an important official at **Knossos**. The villa was built in a high place and enjoyed a fine view, that included twin peaked hills in the foreground and mountains behind. It consisted of about 18 rooms, courtyards and corridors on two storeys, and incorporated 'classic' Minoan religious features, such as pillar crypts *[see box on p.37]*, a domestic shrine *[see box on p.98]* and a tripartite shrine. Also found at the site were wine and olive oil presses, together with a kiln that indicated a potter's workshop. A large clay jug of Vasiliki ware *[see box on p.10]* was found. The villa probably controlled a large area of countryside, and was in use for many years until destroyed by fire at the end of the

Above – Vathypetro villa
Below – view from villa

Neopalatial [LMIB], possibly the 1450BCE conflagration.
From Vathypetro, take the road to **ARKALOCHORI**. There was a sacred cave here, with finds of double axes, now in **Heraklion Museum** *[see p.16]*. About 8km along this road, there is a turning left for Galatas.

GALATAS

An early Neopalatial site may be seen on the hill. This site was modelled on the Palace-Temple sites, with which it had features in common. These included a paved central court, a pillar hall, miniature frescos, storerooms with pithoi, and stones with 'masons marks'. There was also a distinctive baetyl stone *[photo right & see box on p.58]*. To the west of this court were buildings that included rooms for libations and offerings, and finds that included a sealstone depicting an 'ibex-headed woman' flanked by birds. The excavator concluded that this figure was divine and possibly a nature Goddess.

EAST OF HERAKLION

Returning to Heraklion, we now move eastwards along the old (coastal) road to visit other important sites. Passing through the suburbs of **Poros** and **Katsambos** (one of the Knossos harbours) we come after 7km to **AMNISOS** (the other Knossos harbour). Here there are the remains of a Neopalatial villa, named **House of the Lilies**, from the frescos that were discovered there, depicting papyrus, irises, mint and lilies. There were ten rooms on the ground floor, and several more above, which included a shrine *[see box on p.98]* and a lustral basin *[see box on p.38]*. Overlooking the plain of Amnisos, a dwelling was found at **PRASAS**, consisting of at least two buildings (from the Protopalatial and Neopalatial periods) in a very ruined state. However, excavation did reveal that Building A contained a shrine, and cups and jugs (some decorated with double axes), amphora and gournes (stone bowls) were found. Finds from Building B included a libation bowl made of limestone, with Linear A characters carved into the stone. The site (in an olive grove) is now almost completely ruined.

EILEITHYIA CAVE

To the east of Prasas, on a hillslope overlooking the coast, lies the Eileithyia cave. It is a shame that this cave site is no longer open to the public, as it was an important place of worship of the Goddess from the Late Neolithic up until Roman times (5th century CE). The cave is 60m in length, and near the centre is a stalagmite some 150cm tall with a roughly shaped stone in front that was used as an altar. Nearby is another stalagmite, and the two were worhipped as Mother and Daughter, until their heads were chopped off by fanatical Christians in the historical period. The whole cave was sacred to Eileithyia, Goddess of childbirth and divine helper of women in labour, and when excavated in 1929 and 1938, votive offerings of clay figurines to the Goddess were found. The Goddess is mentioned as e-re-u-ti-ja (meaning the goddess Eleuthis) in a Linear B fragment from **Knossos**. The worship of the Goddess at this site was remembered as late as the 8th century BCE, when Homer made reference to it in the *Odyssey*. It is thought that the Goddess known in historic times as Eileithyia can be traced back to a Goddess worshipped in the Minoan period, and before that in Neolithic times, as her name does not appear to be Indo-European in origin. There was another cave devoted to her on the coast in southern Crete *[see p.77]*.

Goddess stalactite in Eileithyia cave

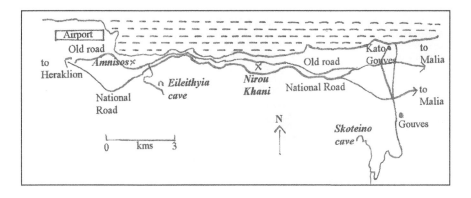

NIROU KHANI

5km east of Amnisos (12km from Heraklion) on the old (coastal) road stands the Minoan house of Nirou Khani, built in the Protopalatial period (MMII). As you enter the house from the eastern side you cross a paved courtyard with raised paths, where fragments of a horns of consecration was found *[see box on p.15]*. This was a large building, with two storeys and 40 rooms on the ground floor. In one of these rooms, four large thin double axes *[see box on p.14]* were found that were doubtless used for ceremonial purposes. Traces of a domestic shrine with a hearth were also identified. In other rooms there were a large number (about 40) of tripod tables for offerings, which has given rise to speculation that the site was used for export of ritual objects through the Minoan harbour of Ayii Theodori nearby. Others have argued that the cult objects were actually used in ceremonies in the East Court of what was clearly an impressive building. Interestingly, a number of votive cups were found containing pieces of volcanic pumice from the Thera eruption *[see p.6]* which had been placed underneath a shrine. It has been suggested that they may have been put there as a re-foundation or reconsecration deposit after the building had been repaired, perhaps from damage caused by a tidal wave from the eruption. In any case, the house underwent substantial structural modifications at this time, before being finally destroyed in LMIB, at the same time as the houses at **Tylissos** and **Sklavokambos**, perhaps by the 1450BCE conflagration.

Travelling further east along the old (coastal) road we reach the seaside resort of Kato (Lower) Gouves, 18km from Heraklion. Here you can turn right and head southwards to the village of Ano (Upper) Gouves. Through the village, take a right hand turn and follow the signs to the sacred cave of Skoteino. Near the entrance of the cave is the church of Aghia Paraskevi, showing that worship at this spot continued into Christian times. Saint Paraskevi is a matron saint of the blind, which would seem to be appropriate for anyone entering the darkness of the cave.

SKOTEINO CAVE

This is a large cave, and as you enter, daylight can be seen above. At this top level, there is a distinctive stalagmite, that has sometimes been identified with Britomartis, a named Goddess from central and eastern Crete, who may be a local variant of the Greek Goddess Artemis. This later named Goddess may have replaced an earlier unknown Goddess, worshipped here in Minoan times, from Protopalatial (MMIB) through Neopalatial and Postpalatial periods into Roman times. This cave is 160 metres deep, and has four distinct levels. The deep descent is only for the confident and well-shod: in particular, the bottom level, reached by a broken ladder, should not be attempted solo. Descending into the total darkness feels very much like going into the womb of mother earth. The cave was first investigated by Evans, and then excavated by Kostas Davaras in 1962. He discovered three Neopalatial bronze votive figurines in the characteristic pose of salutation to the Goddess, with the right hand raised to the forehead *[see photo on p.10]* This cave has long been a powerful sacred place to connect to the Goddess, and continues to hold a numinous power.

SMARI ACROPOLIS

From Skoteino, return to the National Road and head east. At the next major turn south, take the road to Kastelli, where the road turns west. Take the next turn northwards to Smari (23km from Heraklion), and in the village there is a minor road going eastwards and then south to Mt. Profitas Ilias, and the Smari Acropolis. At the top of the hill, a sanctuary has been excavated. At the lower levels, poorly preserved Minoan remains were found from the Protopalatial (Middle Minoan) period, but this was obviously an important site, as later in the Iron Age (Geometric/Orientalising period – 970-650 BCE), a sanctuary to the Goddess Athena Ergani was built there (in a location called Troulli). The excavators thought this was the seat of an important local ruler, who continued with the worship of a Goddess. In the wider area of Smari, the remains of other buildings have also been uncovered, including a vaulted tomb at the hill of Livaditsa.

From Gouves, travel eastwards past **HERSONISOU**, where there was a temple in Classical times to the Goddess Britomartis on the headland.

MALIA

Open: Daily (except Mondays) 0830-1500.
Location: 24km east of Heraklion. The resort of Malia itself may be avoided by taking the National Road, which by-passes the town, and exiting at the far end of Malia, then driving back to the archaeological site, which is signposted. Busses also run from Heraklion to Malia.

Summary: Malia is the third largest of the Palace-Temple sites, and the experience of visiting it is very different to Knossos. Here there are no tour guides to hassle you, and (providing you do not walk on the walls) no site guardians to move you along. You can experience at your leisure the atmosphere of the site, which unlike Knossos, is not rebuilt or over-interpreted.

History of Malia

There was a settlement here as far back as the **Neolithic**, though little trace now remains. However by the **Prepalatial period** [EMIIB] a town had grown up large enough to occupy an area of 2.58 hectares. Remains of this town have been found beneath the temple-palace site and to the north west. Remains of buildings from EMIII to MMIA (end of the Prepalatial period) appear to represent a town considerably larger than anything that existed before. However the later palace-temple has probably covered up most of these remains. Although there is still some debate about the precise timing, it would seem that at the beginning of the **Protopalatial period** (about 1900 BCE, the same time as **Knossos** and the other large palace-temple sites), the first palace-temple site at Malia was built, which has left evidence of a system of paved streets radiating out from the Old Palace buildings. Towards the end of this Protopalatial period, a large complex of administrative buildings and workshops were built to the north-west of the main site (named by the excavators as Quartier Mu – *see p.59*) that have yielded a wealth of finds. The function of this area was connected to the preparation and manufacture of artefacts to be used for ritual and ceremony. About 1700 BCE, an earthquake severely damaged the site (as it did at other palace-temple sites), and a New Palace was built (**Neopalatial period**) which lasted until the 1450 BCE conflagration. It is the remains of this Neopalatial palace-temple site that we can see today. A few parts of the town site were reoccupied in in the **Postpalatial period**, particularly in the Quartier E area *[see p.59]*. Excavation by French archaeologists is continuing at the site.

Plan of Malia

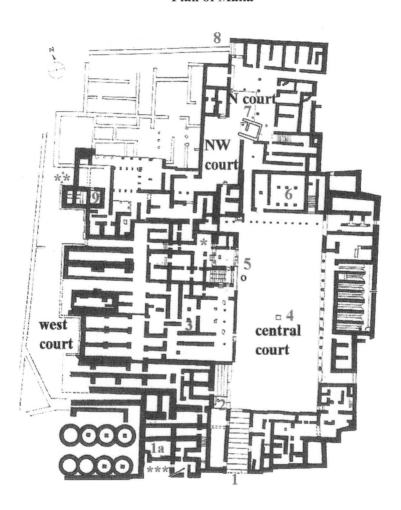

1. South entrance
2. Kernos
4. Sunken altar
6. Pillared hall
8. North entrance & paved road

1a. Shrine
3. Pillar crypt
5. Baetyl
7. Postpalatial shrine
9. Lustral basin

* find place of leopard head axe & bronze sword
** find area of the sword of the acrobat artefact
*** find of altar with signs of star and cross (in 1a. Shrine)

56

Tour of Malia

The layout of Malia is similar to that of **Knossos**, with a Central Court and a paved West Court, the west side of the buildings being used mainly for ceremonial purposes, and the east side mainly for administration. Again, like Knossos, there were two main entrances, one to the north and one to the south. For the purposes of this Tour, we enter from the south. There was one small entrance that originally led to a **shrine** (1a) that may have included a dining shrine *[see box on p.67]* where an altar was found. The other main **entrance** (1) originally would have led leftwards into an antechamber and on to a paved

terrace, from where two steps led on to the Central Court. In the terrace room there is a well preserved limestone **kernos** (offering bowl) (2) *[see box below and photo right]*, which is displayed where it was found. Continuing up the west side of the complex there are a number of labyrinthine rooms (like Knossos), some of which show 'masons marks' of double-axe carvings *[see box on p.14]*, indicating the cultic nature of the rooms. There was a **lustral basin** (9) *[see box on p.38]*, and also a **pillar crypt** (3) *[see box on p.37 & 47 and photo right]*, which would have been a dark enclosed room. It too had double axes carved on the pillar.

KERNOS. A kernos is a cult vessel with a number of receptacles, usually (but not always) round in construction, with the number of receptacles varying from one to another. The one at **Malia** *[above]* is well preserved, with a hollow in the centre and 34 smaller ones around the circumference, although other smaller ones have been found, most notably at **Gournia** and **Phaistos**. Their use is not certain, although there is an illustration of one carried by a Priestess on her head in a procession at the Eleusinian Mysteries, which were held near Athens, presumably as offerings to a Goddess (probably Demeter). Some were found in a temple to Demeter at **Aptera**. Athenaeus, writing at the beginning of the 3rd century CE describes one as holding cereals and honey cakes, and it may well be that they were designed to hold offerings to a harvest Goddess as part of a ritual ceremony.

The Central Court dates back to the Protopalatial period, measures 28m x 22m, and is on the same orientation as the central courts at **Knossos** and **Phaistos**, namely NNE by SSW. This one at Malia however has two interesting features. In the centre there is a shallow pit that was probably an **altar** (4). It was lined with mudbrick, with four mudbrick stands in it. Interestingly, it aligns directly E-W with the Pillar Crypt, so may be connected with ritual activities there. At the NW side of the Central Court, at the bottom of the stairs that led down into the Court from the ceremonial area, there is a **baetyl** stone (5). Baetyls are cult stones *[see box below]* so its positioning there is not a coincidence. Returning to the rooms on the western side, two artefacts were found in the area denoted * on the plan on p.56. One of these was the ceremonial stone axe with the leopard/panther head *[photo on p.11]* dating from the Protopalatial period, which was found hidden in a vase with a bronze bracelet. Also found was a dagger and a sword with rock crystal hilt.

On the north side of the Central Court was a two storeyed room, described as a **pillared hall** (6). Cooking pots were found here, so it may have served as a dining area, similar to one found at **Zakros**. To the north-west of it were two small courts, and wedged between them is a room at an oblique angle to the rest of the rooms. This dates from a much later Postpalatial period [LMII] and is thought to have been a **Postpalatial shrine** (7). At the western fringes of the site another find was made, dating from the Protopalatial period (denoted ** on the plan on p.56). This was the Sword of the Acrobat, a figure arched across a gold disc on the hilt. These exquisite finds from the Protoplatial period show that Malia was a prosperous and artistic centre in the Old Palace period. Finally, we reach the **North entrance** of the site (8) from where a **paved road** ran westwards towards the harbour area.

BAETYLS. Baetyls were described by Evans as "cultic objects that were the subject of veneration (such as pillars, columns and even stalagmites and trees) that seemed to be an aniconic (symbolic or suggestive) representation of a divinity, specifically a Goddess". These objects were worshipped and venerated by the Minoan people as "a material home for the spiritual being, brought down into it by due ritual" – in other words an epiphany of the Goddess *[see box on p.18]*. However, recent researchers have tended to limit them to square, oblong or round stones (dating from Prepalatial right up to Postpalatial times) that were specifically venerated at certain sites in significant places, and a recent study admits only 7 stones from 6 Cretan sites (at **Malia**, **Vasiliki** *[photo on p.89]*, **Ayia Triada tomb**, **Galatas** *[photo on p.51]*, **Gournia** and **Kephala Vasiliki**). They are also depicted on seal stones, where priestesses are shown hugging or reverencing them.

To the NW of the site were several more substantial buildings, which can be visited. Firstly there is the **Agora**, a walled building around a courtyard, with foundations that originally supported banks of seats. We know that it was in use in the Protopalatial period, though its use is unknown. Next to it was the **Hypostyle Crypt**, which consisted of two interconnected halls with benches on three sides. It has been suggested that it was a meeting place for a 'town council'. The most interesting area lies beyond it: the complex of buildings known as **Quartier Mu**. This area represents the town that grew up in the Protopalatial period (concurrent with the first palace-temple site) and was clearly where some of the people lived. There were also workshops turning out artefacts and implements for the site. Two large two-storey buildings have been identified (the largest of which had

Part of Quartier Mu

30 rooms on the ground floor), and one of which had a roofed lustral basin *[see box on p.38]* and a room with a sanctuary beside it. The workshops must have been a hive of activity, with seal engravers, potters and metalworkers turning out some of the practical and prestige goods found in the main site. Many finds were made here too, including cauldrons and a bowl in bronze, ceramic reliefs (one of a sphinx), and ceremonial objects such as a dagger with gold handle. An archive of hieroglyphic inscriptions on tablets, pottery and seals was also found, as well as numerous human and animal figurines, miniature vases and offering tables. This was a productive and busy place, which was destroyed at the end of the Protopalatial period, probably by the 1700 BCE earthquake.

Other outlying areas to the main site are **Quartier Z** to the east, which consists mainly of houses, and **Quartier E** to the south (which is fenced but can be seen from the road to the site). Quartier E was first inhabited in the Neolithic, and then developed in later periods before being abandoned in the Postpalatial period [LM]. There was a large house that had storerooms laid out around a small court, and a metalworker's workshop that contained double axe moulds and a pyramid-shaped double axe stand. Parts of vases decorated with double axe motifs and used for ritual and cult activities were also found. The only examples of frescos in Malia (none in the main palace-temple site) have been found here, in a room connected to a lustral basin. The site has also yielded stone and clay vessels, stone lamps, offering tables, bronze daggers and tools, parts of figurines and seal stones. Across the road remains have been discovered of a **Shrine**, with horns of consecration *[see box on p.15]* incorporated into the building.

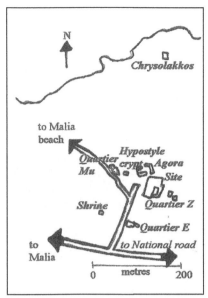

Chrysolakkos – view of the site

Finally, no visit to Malia is complete without going to **CHRYSOLAKKOS**, if only to see where the famous Bee Goddess pendant was found *[see photo on p.11]*. To get to the site, take the road from the main palace-temple site down to Malia beach, and then take a coastal path running north-eastwards for about 500 metres. Chrysolakkos (fenced) is visible on the right hand side of the path.

It consists of a large rectangular enclosure, divided into a number of compartments, with paved areas around the outside. There was a Prepalatial phase, that may have had a funerary function. Most of what can now be seen dates from the Protopalatial period, the time of the building of the first palace-temple site at Malia. It is assumed that it was an ossuary or cemetery of some sort, though it is unlike any such similar one: there were no entrances, and rooms were enclosed without interconnecting doors.

It has been suggested that it was the burial place for high status individuals from the palace-temple site. If this is correct, we may imagine that the bee goddess pendant had been buried with a Priestess who used to officiate at ceremonies in the main site. This interpretation is given some weight by the artefacts that were found here, including a stuccoed altar, lamps, funerary context pottery (including a Goddess libation jug), and clay figurines, all of which are indicative of a cult of the dead *[see box on p.47]*.

Chrysolakkos - aerial view

FOR SITES FURTHER EAST SEE PROVINCE OF Lasithi [p.78 on]

WEST OF HERAKLION

Returning to Heraklion, we now move westwards along the National Highway to **GAZI**, now a modern town but originally the site of the old Minoan harbour of Tylissos. Here was found a Postpalatial shrine, from which came five impressive GUAs (Goddess with Upraised Arms) *[see box on p.23]* including the one popularly known as the 'Poppy Goddess' *[see photos on p.23]*. Gazi is also the home of the Malevizi Collection, a small private collection of Minoan and other artefacts from the area made by Nikolaos Metaxas from 1959 to 1997. The collection is in a building in a public park at the eastern end of the town and is open to the public.

From Gazi, take the road running westwards towards Marathos, and after 3km take a turning south to the major Minoan settlement of Tylissos.

TYLISSOS

Tylissos retains its pre-Hellenic name, which occurs on Linear B tablets as *tu-ri-so*. There was some kind of Prepalatial settlement here, but what remains now are three large interconnected Neopalatial buildings [MMIII to LMIA]. House A in the centre had a small paved court, storerooms and a possible banqueting hall above. In its south wing, there was a lustral basin *[see box on p.38]* and a pillar crypt *[see box on p.37]*, where the excavators found a pyramidal stand for a double axe, similar to one found at **Knossos** and at **Malia (Quartier E)**. To the south of this room were two small storerooms, where three huge bronze cauldrons were found, as well as a bronze figurine and tablets with Linear A inscriptions *[see box on p.12]*. To the west of House A is House B (which may have been an administration and storage area), and to the north of House A is House C, entered from the eastern side. Here there was a cult area, including another pillar crypt and lustral basin. A large collection of miniature frescos was found at this site. The whole complex lay at the base of Pyrgos hill to the NE, which was in use as a Peak Sanctuary during this period *[see box on p.16]*. Many clay figurines of devotees were found there. The buildings were destroyed at the end of the Neopalatial period by the 1450 BCE conflagration, but there was re-occupation in the Postpalatial period, some of whose buildings now cut across the Neopalatial remains. To complicate it further, the site continued in use after the end of the Minoan-Mycenean period, and an independent city state arose here that manufactured its own coins, and worshipped the Goddess Artemis.

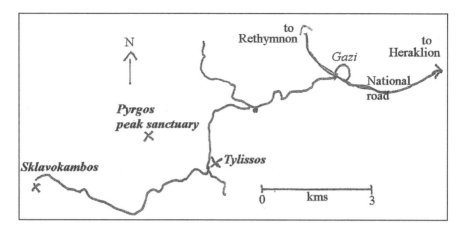

From Tylissos a country road leads westwards for about 5km to the Minoan house of Sklavokambos.

SKLAVOKAMBOS

Sklavokambos is a Minoan villa dating from the Neopalatial period, and was therefore built at the same time as Tylissos. However, unlike Tylissos, the building is cruder in construction, with unpaved floors, though it did have a pillared veranda with a view over the valley, and a small open courtyard with three pillars supporting a peristyle roof (a colonnaded court resembling a cloister). Finds included the clay head of a bull and a stone rhyton. Several clay seals were discovered with bull-leaping scenes, similar to those found at **Aghia Triada**, **Gournia** and **Zakros**.

From Sklavokambos it is possible to travel westwards and southwards into Rethymnon province to view the settlement site of **Zominthos** and the sacred cave at **Mt. Ida (Idean Cave)** *[see next page, and full details*

(Above) Sklavokambos
(Below) Bull-leaping ring

of which can be found on p.113]. Alternatively, return to the National Highway, go eastwards and take the next major road south to **Phaistos**, **Aghia Triada** and the **Mesara tholos tombs** *[see pages 64-76]*.

Mt. Ida was one of the most important mountains in Crete, and at 2456 metres it is the highest peak which dominates much of the surrounding countryside. It is visible from **Phaistos** and many other Minoan sites in the south and west of the island. There was a sacred cave at its summit *[see p.113]*, and also on its southern flank there was another cult cave at **KAMARES**, reached by a steep climb of 4-5 hrs from Kamares village. It gave its name to the large quantities of Kamares ware pottery *[see box on p.10]* that were found here, and some animal figurines and other deposits from the Protopalatial period were also discovered in this cave.

SACRED CAVES. Crete has amost 2000 caves of various shapes and sizes, and many of these were used from the Neolithic period onwards for habitation and burial. Caves at **Gerani**, Miamou ((between **Platanos** and **Lendas** in the south) and Stavomyti at **Mt. Juktas** produced evidence of occupation and use from the late Neolithic period. At **Zakros**, in the Prepalatial period, the dead were buried in the caves lining the gorge. By the Minoan period (Protopalatial and Neopalatial), caves were increasingly being used as foci for religious and spiritual practices. They were often visually connected to the surrounding region, and visible from the nearest settlement, for example the **Kamares** cave, which appears as a black hole in the mountainside that is visible from **Phaistos** and the entire Mesara valley. The caves became the object of pilgrimage, and entering them must have been an intense sensory experience, perhaps enhanced by incense smoke, music and an altered state of consciousness. Within the cave there was a sacred area, where the religious devotions took place, which included the giving of votive offerings. Examples include **Skoteino, Trapeza, Dicktean Cave (Psychro), Arkalochori, Idean Cave, Kamares** and **Melidoni**. At the Dicktean and Arkalochori caves miniature gold and silver double axes *[see box on p.14]* were inserted into niches in the cave walls. and into the stalagmites and stalactites. Caves would have been perceived as a liminal space between the everyday world and the chthonic underworld of the Goddess, and at some caves, such as the **Dicktean cave** and **Skoteino**, bronze figurines were deposited. Many of these figurines, found in caves and at Peak Sanctuaries *[see box on p.16]* show a worshipper in a gesture of adoration or supplication to the Goddess. From evidence on seal rings and other figurines, it has been suggested that the arms folded over the breast indicates a way of achieving states of ritual trance for healing purposes. In later times, the caves continued to be visited to ask the Goddess for her blessings, and some caves were named for her; for example the **Eileithyia** childbirth caves near **Amnisos** and at **Inatos**, and the Cave of Artemis the bear near **Gouverneto**, where stalagmites were thought to be the Goddess incarnate and were worshipped.

SOUTH OF HERAKLION

Returning to Heraklion, take the main road going south (signposted Mires). On the way, south of Venerato is the ancient city state of **RIZENIA** (Prinias), the remains of which lie on an acropolis on a flat-topped hill. There was a Postpalatial [LMIII] sanctuary there, similar to **Gazi** and **Karphi**, from which came a GUA (Goddess with Upraised Arms) figurine *[see box on p.23]*, as well as numerous votive terracottas including snakes and snake tubes, thought to be associated with the cult of the sacred snake *[see photo on p.24]*. The site continued into the Archaic and Hellenistic periods. Further down the road turn west at Aghia Deka, and just outside the town to the north is the Graeco-Roman city state of **GORTYN** (temple to Athena Poliouchos). To the south is the village of Mitropoli, and 2km SW of the village are the remains of a Neopalatial [LMI] villa or farmhouse at **KANIA**. It was destroyed in the 1450 BCE conflagration, but reoccupied in the Postpalatial period when it housed a shrine, where were found more than four GUAs *[see box on p.23]* and three snake tubes. Continue westwards to Mires and then on to the place-temple site of Phaistos.

PHAISTOS

Open: April - end Oct, Daily 0800-2000. Nov - Apr, Daily 0830-1500
Location: 53km south of Heraklion, signposted south of the Mires-Tymbaki road.
Summary: Phaistos is the second largest of the Palace-Temple sites, and has many features in common with **Knossos** and **Malia**. It has the same relationship to the twin-peaked **Mount Ida**, north of the site *[see page.63 &113]* as does Knossos to **Mount Jucktas**, and is a complex site to visit.

History of Phaistos

Phaistos was inhabited in late Neolithic times before the first place-temple was constructed in the early **Protopalatial** [MMIB] period. There are some remains from this period, particularly on the west & NE side of the site, and finds included Linear A tablets, Kamares ware pottery *[see box on p.10]* and the Phaistos Disc *[see p.13]*. A kernos, similar to the one at **Malia** was also found. The Old palace-temple was destroyed by earthquake at the end of MMII, and a new one built on the ruins in the **Neopalatial** period before being destroyed at the time of the 1450 BCE conflagration. Ruins of some of the Old buildings as well as the New can be seen. There is a marked absence of finds from this new site, for example, no frescos, tablets or sealstones (though three figurines were found in the west wing), the reasons for which are not really understood. There was some re-occupation of the site in the **Postpalatial** period, and the ruins were built on again in the Geometric and Hellenistic periods, when a large town existed here.

Plan of Phaistos

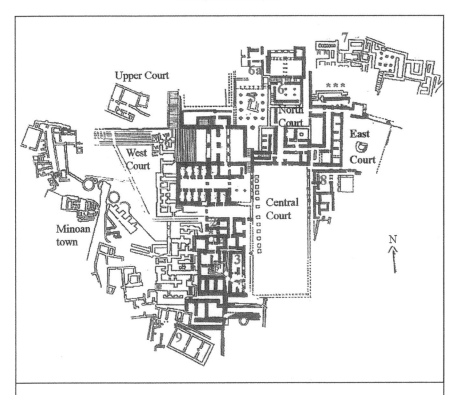

Light type – buildings from Protopalatial (except 9 from Classical period).
Heavy type – buildings from Neopalatial.

1. Shrine area
2. Sanctuary rooms
3. Pillar crypt
4. Lustral basins
5. Peristyle hall
6. Royal apartments
6a. Lustral basin
7. Workshops
8. East wing
9. Temple to Rhea

*   find room of adorant figurines
     (in 2. Sanctuary room)
**   find of Phaistos Disc
     (in 7. Workshops area)
*** find of kernos vessel
     (in area south of Workshops)

Tour of Phaistos

The site is entered from the north, directly into what remains of the first Protopalatial palace-temple. A staircase descends to the West Court, to the right of which are the remains of the old Minoan town, from where were found many vessels of Kamares ware *[see box on p.10]*. To the left, there is a small building that was a **shrine complex** (1) including a Dining Shrine *[see box on p.67]* from the first Protopalatial period. A large clay offering table, stone vases, a triton shell and other cult objects were found there. South of this are the remains of the first palace-temple site (now fenced off for continuing excavation).

To the left (east) there is a broad staircase, an original Minoan structure, that leads into the Neopalatial palace-temple site. There was a monumental Grand Entrance into the site, through a porch with a massive central column, in front of a pair of double doors, leading to a narrow ante-room and a large colonnaded light well. From here steps lead down to the Central Court, which, like the ones at **Knossos** and **Malia**, was oriented NNE-SSW. Unlike those at Knossos, Malia and **Zakros**, however, it does not appear to have had an altar. From the Central Court there is a good view to the sacred twin peaked hill of **Mt. Ida** to the north *[see p.63]*.

On the left (west) side of the Central Court, there are a suite of 4 rooms, very much like those at Knossos and Malia, that seem to have been a sanctuary complex (2). A Goddess and two female adorant figurines were found here. South of this were rooms that were respectively a **pillar crypt** (3) *[see box on p.37]* and two **lustral basins** (4) *[see box on p.38]*, reinforcing the notion that this was a sacred area.

From the north end of the Central Court, there was a passage and a staircase that led to the upper storey, which may have been a dining area, similar to the one at **Malia**. Stairs from the NW corner of the Central Court lead in this direction to the **peristyle hall** (5), in the centre of which are the remains of the foundations of the earlier Prepalatial building. To the north of this are the remains of the so-called **Royal Apartments** (6) which include a hall that contained part of a potter's wheel with an incised double axe *[see box on p.14]* and an area under a staircase where were found two fine rhyta. One had a decoration of religious symbols, such as double axes and sacral knots, and the other a decoration of leaves. There was also a **lustral basin** (6a) *[see box on p.38]* that was relined with gypsum slabs from nearby quarries. The indication is that this area was occupied by important people in the site's organisation, perhaps priestess officiants.

To the NE of the site are a series of **workshops** (7), dating to the earlier Protopalatial period where was found the famous Phaistos Disc *[see p.13]* and a rhyton in the form of a bull. Also from this period, a kernos was found *[see box on p.57]*, similar to the one at **Malia**, though smaller with 14 hollows around a central hollow. Returning to the east side of the site, there is the East Court and the east wing (8) which has domestic quarters, where were found vases, an offering table and bronze double axes. Finally, at the SW corner of the site may be seen the walls of a **temple** (9) of the Classical period, dedicated to the Great Mother Goddess, Rhea.

DINING SHRINES. Dining Shrines are the most common of all the early shrines in Minoan Crete, originating in **Myrtos** in the Prepalatial era. They increased in popularity in the Protopalatial period and continued throughout the Neopalatial. In general, they followed a similar design, and were used in a sacred context, whereby a small number of people could dine with the divinity in order to honour her. Protopalatial dining shrines were bench sanctuaries, which contained benches along its walls for either a small group of chosen people to sit on, or to hold ritual items. They also contained cultic objects, used within a sacred context. At **Phaistos** the dining shrines were built near to the West Court, close to the grain storage silos (kouloures). This may have been deliberate to celebrate grain, bread preparation and the harvest. The one from the Old Palace [(1) on the site plan *p.65*] consisted of 4 rooms that included a food preparation area, containing a mill, water trough and drain. Outside there was a hearth from which animal bones were excavated, indicating the cooking of meat, perhaps from a sacrifice. It is estimated that it could probably seat no more than 15 people, and so it would seem that a small 'invited' group would celebrate within its walls, whilst the rest of the population would join in a public ceremony within the West Court. In the New Palace site at Phaistos, at least one further dining shrine was built, in a suite of 4 rooms facing the West Court [(2) on the site plan *p.65*]. It had a bench shrine, food preparation area and storage rooms. Finds of a Goddess figurine wearing a flounced skirt and two female adorants here reinforce the sacred nature of the dining area. Within other Neopalatial temple-palace sites dining shrines were also evident, for example at **Malia** [(1a) on the site plan p.56]. Once again it was not far from the grain silos (kouloures). **Zakros** also had its dining shrine within the West Wing [(7) on site plan *p.109*]. Here food preparation areas contained benches, grinding stones and a drain. Finds included pottery with a double axe motif and a rhyton. Dining shrines were small exclusive sacred places, unlike Banqueting Halls (usually on upper floors) used for mass secular eating.

AGHIA TRIADA

Open: April - end Oct, Daily (except Monday) 1000-1630. Nov - Apr, Daily (except Monday) 1000-1500
Location: From Phaistos take a minor road west, and after 3km you reach Aghia Triada (also spelt Ayia Triada).
Summary: Aghia Triada is a high status Minoan site. Although not a palace-temple (it has a different layout), nevertheless it was on a par with **Phaistos**, and it may even have seen a transfer of administrative functions and importance away from Phaistos. There are also a wealth of finds from the Neopalatial period that are lacking at Phaistos.

History of Aghia Triada

The site shows continuous occupation from the Neolithic to the end of the Minoan-Mycenean period and beyond. To the north of the site two **Prepalatial** [EMII - MMI] tholos tombs have been discovered *[see box on p.71]*, which held about 150 individual burials, and have yielded grave goods including bronze daggers, jewellery, stone vases, clay pots, and ivory and faience sealstones. The site itself was

built in the **Neopalatial** [LMI] period, contemporary with the palace-temple site at Phaistos, but was destroyed in the 1450BCE conflagration. Finds from this period include frescoes, carved stone vases, bronze figurines, a hoard of 19 copper ingots, and an archive of tablets inscribed in Linear A script. After the conflagration, the site was then rebuilt in the Postpalatial [LMIII] period, during which time it regained its importance and flourished, though clearly under Mycenean control. The Prepalatial tholos tombs were re-used, and in a building attached to tholos B the famous Aghia Triada sarcophagus was found *[see p.24-5]*.

Plan of the site

The site looks quite confusing, with no on-site guiding or interpretation boards. A simplified plan on the next page gives the basic outline of the site and the different areas. The Neopalatial buildings formed an L-shape, and included courtyards, residential quarters, storage rooms and shrines. The site was built over in part and also extended northwards in the Postpalatial era, and by the end a large open-air shrine had been built.

The modern entrance to the site leads in to the Postpalatial village area, so for the Neopalatial buildings it is best to go to the SW corner of the L-shape, where there was a Minoan villa and **residential quarters** (1). Here there are rooms that were given over to food preparation and **storage** (2). In one of the rooms were found pottery, an adorant figurine, stone and clay lamps and two bronze cauldrons, one inside the other.

Also found here were jugs, including one with double axe carvings *[photo right]*, the harvester vase, depicting a rural religious procession, and a rhyton decorated with scenes of boxing and bull leaping. These had probably fallen from an upper story. In another room, which may have been a shrine, a fresco was found of a cat stalking a partridge, together with some female figurines.

Moving further eastwards, there is a megaron (an imposing hall) from the Postpalatial period that was built on top of the earlier Neopalatial rooms. On the east side of the site, there are several

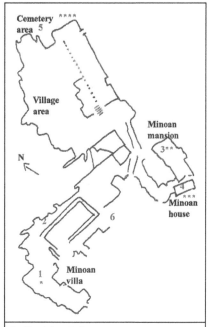

1. *Residential quarters*
2. *Storage area*
3. *Minoan mansion*
4. *Minoan house*
5. *Cemetery area*
6. *Open air shrine*
*   *finds of harvester vase and*
      boxer rhyton
**   *find of bronze double axe*
***   *remains of maritime fresco*
**** *find of sarcophagus*

Neopalatial houses (3) & (4), that produced finds. In one of these (Casa Est) (3) was found several pithoi. Two dagger blades and a bronze double axe were found underneath two of the vessels. The Minoan house (4) had been cut into by the vestibule of a shrine of the Postpalatial period. The floor had remains of a fresco with a maritime theme, featuring dolphins and octopi.

Outside the perimeter of the main site to the NE lay the cemetery area (5) with two tholos tombs, where the Postpalatial sarcophagus was found *[see p.24-5]*. Finally, at the very end of the Postpalatial period, after the destruction of the megaron, the area in front was turned into a **shrine** (6) where female figurines with prominent breasts and snakes were found.

KOMMOS

Returning to **Phaistos**, continue 3km south and take the turning on your right towards the coastal resort of Matala. After another 3 km look for a track on your right (west) at **Pitsidia**, where remains of a Neopalatial villa were found. The turn goes down to the sea at Kommos, which overlooks a sweeping bay and was the Minoan harbour town for Phaistos and Aghia Triada. At that time the sea was 2m

lower and the shoreline extended for a further 50-100m, with a reef offshore to break the waves, so this was a relatively safe anchorage. It was founded in the Protopalatial period [MMIB], and by the Neo-palatial period densely packed houses covered the hill slope. There were two adjoining monumental buildings, covering an area of 6000 sq.m, which was almost as large as Phaistos. In the

Postpalatial period a building with six galleries, which may have been boatsheds, was constructed on top of the Neopalatial site. It thrived throughout this period, showing that contact between Crete and overseas lands (particularly with Cyprus, Syria, Egypt and Italy) was flourishing. The settlement was not abandoned until the late Postpalatial period [LMIIIB], and after that a number of temples were built in subsequent eras. One of these may have been built by Phoenicians in 8thC BCE (where was found a faience figurine of Sehkmet, the lion-headed Egyptian Goddess, with a cat (Bast?) at her feet); and another in the 4thC BCE (where the base of a statue was found that probably held a cult statue of a deity).

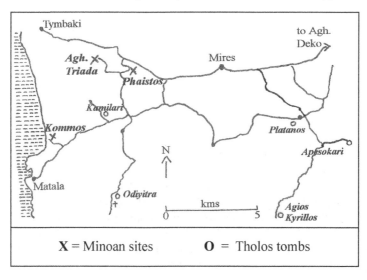

MESARA THOLOS TOMBS

This area of south central Crete provides rich pickings for anyone interested in the tholos tombs of the Minoan and Mycenean periods. Some 40 or so tombs are still extant, in various states of preservation, and a handful of the most accessible and worth visiting are given on the following pages, with a location map on p.76.

THOLOS TOMBS. Tholos tombs are freestanding domed-shaped structures, from 4 to 13 metres wide, with thick corbelled walls and vaulted ceilings. Many have annexes (a complex of rectangular rooms) attached to the wall near the entrance, which usually faces east, the direction of the rising sun. These tombs are mainly located around the Mesara Plain, with the earliest examples flanking the southern slopes of the Asterousia mountains. There are over 70 tholos tombs, located in more than 45 villages, mainly in southern Crete. Tholos tombs were in use for over 1000 years: examples from Lebena date from the final Neolithic period, whilst the Kamilari tombs were in use up until the Postpalatial period. It was suggested by Brannigan & Blackman (who excavated the Ayiofarango valley in southern Crete) that tholos tombs were built very close to Prepalatial contemporary settlements and were used by small family groups. Most tombs were used for decades, if not centuries, resulting in hundreds of burials, various grave goods and masses of bones. There is evidence that the tombs were fumigated periodically by the use of fire, and burials were separated by the use of sand being placed on the floor to cover older burials. Within the tholos tombs, primary burials would take place. Here the recently deceased would be interred with their belongings (grave goods) and food and drink to see them to the afterlife. Grave goods found within tholos tombs included: pottery, cups, dishes, libation vessels, tools, jewellery (some in rock crystal, faience and gold), daggers (made of copper and bronze and occasionally silver), sealstones, and anthropomorphic and zoomorphic ceramic vessels. Those goods that have a particular religious or ritual significance include Cycladic-style female figurines (Goddesses?), kernoi *[see box on p.57]*, (which in the tholos tombs are usually rectangular with three or four holes and have incised designs on them), and, in three particular sites, (**Kamilari**, **Platanos** & **Apesokari**) bronze double axes. Once the corpse became skeletal, a principle bone would be removed from the tholos, and placed into a communal ossuary as a secondary burial. Many tholos tombs were overseen by 'cult of the dead' priestesses/priests *[see box on p.47]* who were responsible for funerary and ritual celebrations: examples include sites at **Phourni** and **Achladia**. Tholos tombs are magnificent structures, which honoured the dead long before the majestic palace-temples were built, and continued in use during and after their construction.

KAMILARI THOLOS TOMB

Directions: From the Phaistos to Matala road take the Kamilari turning at the Sivas crossroads, and follow signs to the tomb, which lies in an olive grove. The

tomb is located on a low hill, and is the largest and best preserved of three tholos tombs found in the area when Italian archaeologists carried out excavations in the area at the end of the 1950s. The tomb was built in the Protopalatial [MMIB] period and continued in use until early in the Neopalatial [MMIII] period. It was also re-used for a time in the Postpalatial period. The site consists of a round (now roofless) tholos tomb with attached funerary buildings. The tholos is 7.65m in diameter and the walls still stand to a height of 2m in places. It has a built entrance with a large capstone, and the annex to the east of the tomb contains five rooms used for cult purposes. Remains of about 2500 vases of various kinds, including 800

conical cups used for libation ceremonies, were found. Also, dating from the Postpalatial period, three interesting clay models were found, illustrating different aspects of the funerary rite. Two show ritual feasting, including the placing of offerings to the dead on small altars. The third one *[photo right]* shows a group of dancers in a circle, with horns of consecration *[see box on p.15]* and doves to emphasise the ritual setting of the events.

ODIYITRIA THOLOS TOMBS

Directions: From the Phaistos to Matala road, take the turning southwards to the village of Sivas. From here continue southwards until you come to the Odiyitria monastry. Just before the monastry beside the road are the tholos tombs.

There are two tombs (Tholos A & B) that both date from the Prepalatial [EMI] period. They continued in use throughout the Protopalatial period, at the end of which their use was discontinued, with a final closing ceremony.

Tholos A yielded finds of pottery vessels, a bronze knife and a pendant and necklaces. Tholos B was more elaborate and had a second retaining wall built around it not long after it was constructed. A rectangular building, abutting the second outer wall, was also added. It originally contained six rooms, but was subsequently remodelled to contain three. Although the tholos had been badly looted, it still showed fragments of pottery vessels, stone vases, seals, amulets, necklaces, two gold diadems, part of a human figurine made from ivory, one faience figure of a turtle, five bronze daggers and other personal items. Between the two tholoses was an ossuary pit, and outside the tholoses were specially constructed courtyards, that may have been used for funerary rites. Finds made from these areas included vases and animal figurines.

(above) Tholos A and (below) Tholos B

PLATANOS THOLOS TOMBS

Directions: Platanos village lies SE of Mires. Take the turn off the main road to the east of Mires to go directly to the village. It can also be reached by means of a network of local roads from the Phaistos to Matala road.

There were originally three tholos tombs here, but only two now remain, both dating from the Prepalatial period. They are however the largest yet found in the Mesara. Tholos A [EMII] is less well preserved, but finds included bronze daggers and gold ornaments. The tomb had an annex where many more bodies were found. Tholos B [EMIII] has been partly reconstructed, but fines were much poorer here. It too had an annex, used either for burials or for storing stone vessels. Outside the tholos tombs were found small square buildings that were probably ossuaries where the bones from the tombs were deposited to make way for fresh burials.

Tholos B at Platanos

APESOKARI THOLOS TOMBS

Directions: From Platanos take a road SE of the village towards the Asterousia mountains. At the next junction (before the village of Plora) take the left hand fork to the village of Apesokari. Continue on the road to Lendas, and a few hundred metres outside Apesokari there is a signpost for walking to the site. There were two tholos tombs here dating from the Prepalatial period [EMII], together with an annex of 9 rooms that was built about 800 years later [MM]. The site is not well preserved, but the views from here are magnificent. The tombs and annex had been thoroughly looted by the time they were excavated, but there was evidence of many burials and fragments of cups, jugs and cooking vessels, and bronze double axes.

OTHER THOLOS TOMBS IN THE AREA

AGIOS KYRILLOS Directions: Return to Plora, and take the road running south. After nearly 5km you come to the village of Agios Kyrillos, where the late Prepalatial [MM] tholos may be found on the hillside. Unlike other tholos tombs, this one was sunk into the ground and built into the hillside. It retains its trilithon entrance, and has an attached rectangular building. Finds from the outer chambers produced several stone and clay cups, a bull rhyton and the clay statuette of a Minoan male.

LENDAS (Lebena) Directions: Return to Plora and take the Apesokari road south to the coast at Lendas. Here there is a Minoan settlement on the inland slope of Cape Lendas, and in the vicinity five large Prepalatial [EM-MM] tholos tombs. One lies east at **Zervous** (Lebena III), and two (belonging to the settlement on the promontory) are just west of Lendas at **Papoura** (Lebena I & IB). Finds included a gold diadem, two Cycladic figurines, beads and seals, a kernos and an Egyptian scarab. Continuing westwards, the minor road goes towards **Yerokambos** where to the right of the coast road a pair of tombs can be found, one much larger than the other, and a suite of attached rooms (Lebena II & IIa). Lebena II produced beads from necklaces, two bronze daggers, and some zoomorphic figurines, and in both Lebena II & IIa models of scarabs were found. Blackening of the underside of the capstone of Lebena II paints a vivid picture of people entering the tomb bearing the bodies for burial, lit by the fire of flaming torches. Food offerings had been left for the dead, and the lids removed so that the dead could more easily eat or drink.

KOUMASA THOLOS TOMBS

Directions: Koumasa is about 6km SE of Apesokari, but the route is very circuitous. Follow the road to Vagiona, which can also be reached by taking a turn south off the main road at Agh. Deka *[see map on p.76]*. From Vagiona continue SE to Loukia crossroads and then take the right turn towards Koumasa. The tholos tombs are between Loukia and Koumasa.

The site conists of three tholos tombs (A, B & E) and a rectangular tomb G. The tombs were built in the Prepalatial period [EMIIA] and continued in use until the end of that period [MMIA], and have produced a wealth of grave goods, including six Cycladic Goddess figurines. Tholos B is the largest of the group (outside diameter 13.5m) and has given the greatest finds. Hundreds of people were buried in the tomb over a long period

Tholos B at Koumasa

of time, and although many goods had been plundered, there was still much of interest found. These included seven stone objects like small tables, which could have been offering tables. There were also three cylindrical pyxides (small lidded boxes), a number of jugs, anthropormorphic and zoomorphic vases and lamps, 80 stone vases, a snake tube *[see p.24]*, a square kernos with 4 indentations *[see box on p.57]*, 20+ copper daggers, a gold pendant in the shape of a squatting toad, and three gold beads from necklaces. Two of the six Cycladic Goddess figurines came from Tholos B: all 6 were carved in marble and probably imported from the Cyclades. There were also 3 figurines carved from rough limestone, which may have been manufactered in Crete. The excavator of the site Xanthoudides suggested that they represented Mother Goddesses, and had probably been used as sacred figures of worship prior to their burial.

There was a Minoan settlement to the east of the cemetery on a twin peaked hill called Korakies, but nothing remains of it today. About 6km further east, there was the Peak Sanctuary *[see box on p.16]* of **KOFINAS** *[photo right]* that has yielded finds of seals, figurines, a bull rhyton and a Linear A inscribed bronze vessel. This would have been the place to which the inhabitants of the Minoan settlement made pilgrimages.

Kofinas Peak Sanctuary

APODOULOU THOLOS TOMB

Directions: Returning to the main road at Ag. Deka, turn west and go through Mires and past the turn for **Phaistos** and **Aghia Triada** until you reach the town of Tymbaki. Continue on the main road for 7km and then take a right turn on to the road to Fourfouras. After 5km you will come to the village of Apodoulou (in Rethymnon province but included here for the sake of completeness). Through
the village on a bend beside the road stands the tholos tomb (one of 3 that were here) It is unusual in being of Postpalatial date, rather than Prepalatial as are most of the tholos tombs of the Mesara Plain, and in having the lintel and structure above still in place. It is also different in that it has a dromos (entrance walkway) and it is built into the hillside. The tomb had been plundered before excavation, but 4 clay larnakes (clay coffins) were found, one with a scene of lamenting figures, as well as jewels and a necklace with Linear A inscription.

LOCATION OF THOLOS TOMBS ON THE MESARA PLAIN

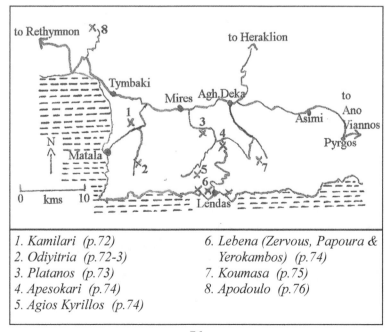

1. Kamilari (p.72)
2. Odiyitria (p.72-3)
3. Platanos (p.73)
4. Apesokari (p.74)
5. Agios Kyrillos (p.74)
6. Lebena (Zervous, Papoura & Yerokambos) (p.74)
7. Koumasa (p.75)
8. Apodoulo (p.76)

APODOULOU MINOAN SETTLEMENT

Also near Apodoulou, there is a substantial Minoan settlement. At the village take a left hand turn towards the village of Aghia Paraskevi. After 1km, the remains of the settlement lie on a hill beside the road.

The site shows a long occupation from the late Neolithic to the end of the Protopalatial period, but chiefly flourished during the Protopalatial period. Altogether, six buildings, covering an area of over 600 sq. metres, have been excavated. These were the residential quarter, and are composed of warehouses, workshops, kitchens and residential rooms. There was also a large courtyard. Finds included stone tools, pottery, pithoi, and hearths with tripod pots, whose contents contained traces of various plants, fruits and leafy vegetables. There was also a room, where remains of rhytons were found, which was interpreted as a shrine room *[see box on p.98]*. The site was destroyed by earthquake and fire at the end of the Protopalatial period, but was reoccupied again in the Neopalatial, where a cult area produced finds of gold and bronze double axes and a bulls head rhyton.

To the NW of Apodoulou is the important site of Monastiraki, which lies nearer to Rethymnon, and is therefore included in the Western section [see page 117-8].

INATOS & KEFALI

Finally, in this Central Crete section, there are two sites to be mentioned in the south-east. Firstly there is **INATOS**, which lies on the south coast at Tsoutsouros (to the SE of Pyrgos). This was a cave (not now accessible), sacred to the Goddess Eileithyia, similar to the one on the north coast east of Heraklion *[see p.52]*. It has yielded evidence of activity from the Minoan to the Roman period. Finds included a Neopalatial stone altar, several bull figurines and double axes *[see box on p.14]*, as well as a large number of terracotta figurines depicting fertility and safe delivery of children. There may also have been a temple to Eileithyia at the top of the hill leading

down to the village, where the chapel of Aghia Eleni now stands. Secondly, about 10km to the NE, near the village of Hondros lies the Postpalatial [LMIII] refuge site of **KEFALI** *[photo right]*. A shrine was found here, with fragments of ritual objects. Both these sites are potent reminders of the enduring power of the Goddess in Crete.

EASTERN CRETE [Lasithi province] – map

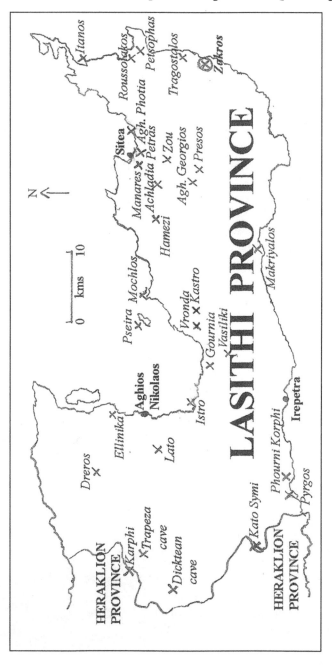

EASTERN CRETE
[Province of Lasithi]

The area of Eastern Crete covers all of Lasithi Province, which is bisected by the road that links the north and south coasts at the shortest distance in Crete (14km) from Pachia Ammos to Irepetra. To the west of this road is the Lasithi Plateau, with the refuge site of Karphi and the Dicktean and Trapeza caves, and the Minoan settlements of Pyrgos and Phourni Korphi. The Sanctuary of Hermes and Aphrodite at Kato Symi was first occupied in Minoan times and lasted well into the Roman period, and many of the other sites, such as Dreros, Ellinika and Lato, are from the end of the Minoan period and into the era of city states. Nevertheless they all have Goddess associations in one way or another. From the road going east lie many more important Minoan settlement sites, such as Gournia, Vasiliki, Petras and Roussalakkos; cemetery sites such as Mochlos and Aghia Photia; peak sanctuaries such as Petsophas and Tragostalos; refuge sites such as Praisos and Kastro; houses and villas such as Hamezi, Achladia and Makriyalos; and the final palace-temple site of Zakros. Here at the far eastern edge of Crete we can look back over a Province rich in sacred sites and Goddess-inspired finds.

LASITHI PLATEAU. The Lasithi Plateau is one of the most oldest inhabited parts of Crete, and until relatively recently, one of the most isolated. It lies at an altitude of 850m in a basin surrounded by tall mountains to the SE of the coastal strip of the Bay of Malia, and to the SW of the historic town of Neapoli. Recent analysis of DNA from remains of 37 ancient people found buried in the Aghios Charalembos cave on the plateau revealed that the plateau has been inhabited continuously since the late Neolithic, with its population reaching an apex in the Protopalatial [Middle Minoan] period, around 1800 BCE. The cave was used as an ossary during all this period, and was then sealed for a number of centuries, which, because of the low temperatures of the cave, helped to preserve the remains. Because of its isolated position, the plateau served as a refuge from invading forces into Crete, and by comparing the DNA of these remains with the DNA of modern Lasithi dwellers, the study was able to show an almost unbroken sequence. Therefore it could be said that the modern day Lasithi people are the last remnants of the Minoan people themselves. The plateau has been farmed continuously since ancient times, as it is a very fertile basin (at one time there were thousands of windmills supplying irrigation to the area), and evidence of Minoan use can be found in the caves of **Dickti** and **Trapeza**, as well as the late Minoan refuge site of **Karphi**.

KARPHI

From Malia a road winds its way up to the Lasithi plateau (joined part way by a road from Hersonnisou that is signposted from the National Highway). About half way along the road, it goes through the small village of Krasi, where a Postpalatial tomb discovered by Evans was excavated in 1929. The road continues upwards, and as it approaches the plateau, there are good views on the left of Karphi, that stands out as a protruding rock on the horizon *[photo right]*. A good place to stop and get a look is at the Museum of Mankind, from where you can ascend to the rock, though this is not an easy route, and not to be recommended. Instead, continue by road on to the junction to the plateau and turn left for the village of Tzermiado. Here a rough track leads northwards to the Nisimou Plateau, from where you can park (near an isolated church) and walk up an ascending waymarked path to Karphi, which passes by a group of 4 small tholos tombs on the way up to the site.

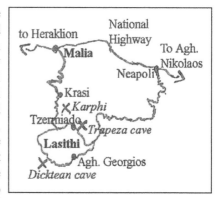

The site is 1100m above sea level, and was chosen as a refuge site by the EteoCretans at the end of the Postpalatial period [LMIIIC], who continued to practice Minoan religious traditions.

There was a civic shrine or temple built at the edge of the precipice, including a large room where remains of an altar were found. Finds from here included six GUAs (Goddesses with Upraised Arms) *[see box on p.23]*, one of which was nearly 1m tall with birds perching in her crown *[now in Heraklion Museum – see p.22]*. Also found was a rhyton (libation jug) in the form of a chariot driven by three oxen heads. There was a sizeable community living here, and it is rather poignant to think of them living out the last days of the Minoan civilisation, maintaining their culture and Goddess religion here in this remote spot for something like 150 years, before abandoning the site.

THE TRAPEZA CAVE

From Tzermiado, there is a sign to the Trapeza cave, which is a steep climb from the village. This is a small cramped cave, that has traces of late Neolithic activity, which continued in use in Minoan times. In the Prepalatial period [EMII] it was in use for communal burials, and a quantity of grave goods were found, including sealstones, rings and other jewellery, figurines, metalwork, stone vases and a glazed steatite scarab. The site was abandoned at the beginning of the Neopalatial period [MMIII]. A Minoan settlement has been excavated nearby at Papoura, which lies in the hills behind the neighbouring village of Lagou.

THE DICKTEAN CAVE

Returning to the junction of the road to the Lasithi plateau from Malia and Hersonisou, carry straight on to the Dicktean cave at Psychro (or if you are coming from Malia or Hersonnisou turn right at the junction). The Dicktean cave is a major tourist destination, and you will most likely find the car park full of tourist buses and cars. There are two alternative steep paths up to the cave, one from the middle of the car park and one from the near end, but if you do not want to climb one of the steep paths, there are donkeys for hire to take you up. Despite the large numbers of visitors to the site, there is a real sense of this having been a sacred cave in Minoan times. The site was visted as early as the late Neolithic period (pot sherds have been found) and continued in use throughout the whole Minoan period, with the peak of activity from the Protopalatial period [MMIIB] onwards. The archaeologist A.S.Vassilakis says that it was "a cult cave where the Mother Goddess was worshipped". Entry into the cave leads into an upper chamber that has a natural hall, which had a rectangular stone shrine. Nearby was a deep crevice in the rock, that may have been part of the ritual use of the area. Votive items including limestone and serpentine offering tables were found there. Steps then lead down to the lower chamber, a huge cavern with beautiful stalagmites and stalactites. At the bottom there is a small pool of water (which would have been deeper in the past), from which were recovered many votive offerings, including bronze statuettes, knives, spearheads and double axes *[see box on p.14]*, most of which dated from the Neopalatial period [LMI]. Arthur Evans visited this cave, and many of finds from the cave can now be found in the Ashmolean Museum in Oxford. To the left of the pool is a small recess (now closed off) which legend says was the place where the Goddess Rhea gave birth to the infant Zeus.

SITES FROM THE ARCHAIC & HELLENISTIC PERIODS

Returning to the National Road, and heading eastwards towards Aghios Nikolaos, a turning north leads to **MILATOS**. This village has a long history, starting with Minoan occupation. There was a settlement here and Postpalatial [LMIII] tholos tombs with cist-shaped larnakes have also been found. The settlement later developed into a city state that lasted until destroyed in the 3rd century CE.

Back on the National Road, take the turning to the town of Neapoli, from where there are signposts 2km to the east for **DREROS**, a city state of the Geometric and Archaic periods (8th-5th centuries BCE). It may have been first occupied in the sub-Minoan period, and remnants of old Minoan customs and traditions may have continued into the later periods. A Temple dated to the Geometric period was found, one of the earliest to be excavated. Finds included a 6th century BCE gorgon mask, vases and figurines, including three bronze statues representing Apollo and Artemis with their mother Leto *[see below]*. It is possible that the last of the Minoans lingered here, as they did at **Praisos**, further east.

Back on the National Road, continue towards Aghios Nikolaos, and at a crossroads outside the town, take a right turn to Kritsa for the city state of **LATO**, named after the Goddess Leto. This site sits in a saddle between two dramatic peaks. There are traces of Postpalatial [LMIII] occupation, but the city state was founded at the end of the Geometric period and continued into the Archaic and Hellenistic. It is well preserved, and remains have been excavated of a court and an agora (public square), where figurines were found from an open-air shrine or temple. A cistern, streets and buildings may also be seen. The religious focal point was a civic temple, dedicated to the Goddess Eileithyia *[see p.52 & 77]*, with the base for a statue of the deity nearby; and a prytaneum dedicated to the Goddess Hestia *[see box on next page]* This was a late site that still worshipped the Goddess.

THE SACRED HEARTH AT CITY STATES. Most City States in the Hellenistic period were considered to be an extended version of the individual home, and therefore each city had its own sacred hearth, the symbol of a harmonious community of citizens and a common worship. The public hearth usually existed in the prytaneum of a town, where the Goddess had her special thalamos (sanctuary) with a statue and a sacred hearth. The Goddess who usually presided over these prytaneums and was invoked there with offerings and prayers was Hestia. She was the Goddess of hearth and home, and also presided over the cooking of bread and the preparation of meals. A new home was not considered established until a woman brought fire from her mother's hearth to light her own, and when a new city or town was established, fire had to be brought from the previous dwellings and made sacred to Hestia in the new city. This fire was never allowed to go out, and had to be tended day and night, as it was considered to be the sacred heart and hearth of the city state. Because Hestia was thought to dwell in the heart of every hearth and town, there were few special temples dedicated to her, but instead it was thought that she was the presiding deity over the pryteaneum and thus of the city state itself. This was the case at **Lato**, **Dreros** and **Rizenia (Prinias)**.

AGHIOS NIKOLAOS AREA

North of Aghios Nikolaos, on the road to Elounda, is the village of **ELLINIKA**. Take the side road leading inland to the remains of a Hellenistic [2nd century BCE] temple, dedicated to Ares and Aphrodite. This small porticoed temple, built of local limestone, consisted of two chambers each with a bench altar, but no connecting door between them. Several carved stones still remain 'in situ', one bearing Aphrodite's name. The site was fought over between the city states of **Lato** and **Olous.**

In Elounda itself we have reached the site of the ancient city state of **OLOUS**, but no remains of it are visible – for it is all underwater! There was a Minoan presence here in the Neopalatial [MMIII] period, but it was in the Hellenistic period that it became a great city state. There was a temple dedicated to Zeus Talaios and to Britomartis, who was a local Goddess, equated with Diktynna *[see p.130]*. A xoanon (an image carved in wood) of the Goddess was housed there. Her effigy was also represented on the coins of Olous, and the festival of Britomarpeia was held in her honour. Over time, the sea levels have risen here, and the remains of Olous have sunk beneath the waves, with pieces of masonry and some inscribed stonework occasionally being recovered.

AGHIOS NIKOLAOS ARCHAEOLOGICAL MUSEUM

Open: Daily (except Mondays) 0830-1500
Location: 74 Konstantinou Palaiologou Str. (north of the lake in the town).

The newly-refurbished Museum consists of 8 rooms, displaying fairly recent finds, mostly from eastern Crete. Details of the most interesting and significant of these are given below.

Room 1 (Neolithic to Prepalatial). This room contains a Neolithic limestone idol from the cave of **Pelekita** (near Zakros), and pottery from the Prepalatial cemetery at **Aghia Photia** (near Sitea). These include goblets, chalices and multiple vases with incised decorations. Bronze blades from the cemetery are also displayed.

Room 2 (Prepalatial to Protopalatial). This room displays finds from the Prepalatial cemetery on the island of **Mochlos**, including delicate gold jewellery (hairpin and gold diadem) folded in a silver box. The famous Goddess of Myrtos (from the **Phourni Korphi** site) is also displayed here, along with other finds from the site, including potters wheels, seals and figurines. The room also has a good display of Vasiliki ware *[see box on p.10]* and Minoan stone vases. There is also a display of clay sistra (percussion instruments like a rattle), which were found in the Aghios Charalembos cave on the Lasithi plateau *[see box on p.79]*.

Goddess of Myrtos

Room 3 (Neopalatial and Postpalatial). This room contains votive offerings from Peak Sanctuaries *[see box on p.16]*, in particular from **Petsophas** near Palaikastro. Also from this site are displayed composite horns of consecration in lime plaster *[see p.105 & box on p.15]*. There are some fine examples of pottery on display, including a triple vessel used in ritual and ceremony from the cemetery at **Myrsini**, and pottery decorated with marine motifs found near **Makriyalos**. A gold pin with Linear A writing *[see box on p.12]* is also displayed.

Postpalatial triple cult vessel and birds from the Myrsini cemetery

Room 4 (mainly Postpalatial). This room contains clay larnakes (burial coffins), and funeral urns, many decorated in the marine style with sea creatures including octopi, which may have been a symbol of regeneration. Interestingly, some of the funeral urns from this late period, at sites such as **Karphi**, still have the Minoan bull's horn motif. There are also a selection of grave goods, including jewellery and combs, from the cemetery at **Milatos**.

Room 5 (Postpalatial). This room has finds from the cemeteries at **Myrsini**, **Lato** and **Gournia**, and includes a child burial in a pithos from the cemetery of Krya, near Sitea. It raises questions about whether burials of

Statue of worshipping female from Myrsini

humans should be dug up and displayed in museums. The room also displays an incense burner and a stand with painted horns of consecration *[see box on p.15]* from the cemetery of **Gra Lygia** near Irepetra on southern Crete.

Room 6 (Archaic). A large collection of finds from a shrine deposit discovered near the centre of modern Sitea.

Room 7 (Hellenistic). Finds from the city state of **Olous**, including votive deposits.

Room 8 (Roman).

FROM AGHIOS NIKOLAOS TO IREPETRA

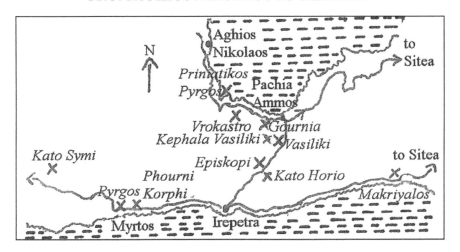

PRINIATIKOS PYRGOS

From Aghios Nikolaos take the main road around the Gulf of Mirabello to the resort of Istro. Before entering Istro, take a side turning down to the coast, and on a small promontory just before where the Istron river flows into the sea, is the archaeological site of Priniatikos Pyrgos. Since 2007, the site has been excavated by an international team under the auspices of the Irish Institute of Hellenic Studies, and they have discovered a site spanning some 4000 years, from the final Neolithic period (c.3000 BCE) through the Minoan period and into the Classical Greek and Roman times, with most of the finds from the Neopalatial period [MMIII - LMI]. A probable Minoan workshop area was discovered, and there were two kilns, similar to ones found at **Kommos**, showing that Priniatikos Pyrgos was a probable pottery production centre and coastal distribution point.

Finds included stone tools, obsidian, part of a bronze pin, and fine-ware cups. Vasiliki ware pottery was found *[see box on p.10]*, including small jars and jugs, bowls, conical and footed globular cups, trays, and larger storage shapes. The fragments include one with breast-like protrusions, and a long neck shape that could have been part of a Goddess figurine. Also found was the clay model of a boat, and paving made of green schist was revealed, with one paving stone having an incised kernos *[see box on p.57]*.

Pottery fragments from the site

VROKASTRO

Above Istro, on a limestone outcrop 313m above sea level, lies the late Minoan refuge site of Vrokastro [12th-7th centuries BCE]. At a similar period and type of location to the refuge sites of **Karphi** and **Kastro**, the site was occupied for some 500 years at the end of the Postpalatial period, presumably by the last of the Minoan peoples. The site consists of a number of houses on an upper and lower level, around a hilltop peak, and running down a north terraced slope. Column bases have been found, indicating that there may have been a communal hall of some sort. Remains of shrines have also been found, together with a bronze GUA, showing that there continued to be a religious element in this settlement site: it is entirely possible that the worship of the Minoan Goddess continued in places such as these. A cemetery was found nearby, that consisted of rock-cut corbel-vaulted tombs, along with pithoi and walled enclosures. Finds from the site show that the site was not completely isolated, with pottery and artefacts coming from the Cyclades, the Dodecanese and mainland Greece.

GOURNIA

Continuing through Istro and around the Bay of Mirabello, the road comes to the important Minoan town of Gournia (20km from Aghios Nikolaos), built on the side of a hill running down to the shore. It formerly occupied an area of about 4 hectares, so what can be seen now is only a proportion of what was originally there. The town originally continued right down to the shore, and excavation of this area is continuing.

There was occupation here in the late Neolithic and Prepalatial [EMII-III] periods, but it was in the Protopalatial that a town of some 400 or so people was established. Around 1700 BCE (perhaps as a result of an earthquake) the town was rebuilt, in the style of a palace-temple site. It had a town court, a narrow cobbled west court, a small 'palace' building (with a lustral basin) and, on the western side,

[above] general view of site
[below] view from pavement on site
over Bay of Mirabello

a cult area. This contained sacred objects including a stone kernos *[see box on p.57]*, a stone with a double axe carving *[see box on p.14]* and a baetyl *[see box on p.58]*. All these remain in situ and can be seen today. The rest of the site has well-preserved buildings, and at its height a population of several thousand people. The buildings would originally have been two storeys high, but now only the ground floor or basement remains. Nevertheless this is an atmospheric site to wander around and get a real sense of where Minoan people lived and worked, and how the everyday and the sacred were so closely linked.

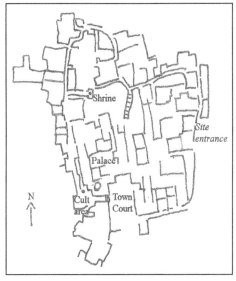

The site was destroyed in the 1450 BCE conflagration, but there was limited reoccupation in the Postpalatial [LMIII] period. A new shrine room was constructed, to the north of the site, approached by three steps. It had a ledge on the south side for the placing of ritual objects. Finds from this room included a low tripod altar in clay, Goddesses with Upraised Arms *[see box on p.23]*, clay tubes with snakes modelled in relief *[photo right & p.24]*, a sherd with a double axe in relief, and bird figurines and serpents' heads modelled in relief. The room is well signed with drawings of the finds, including the GUAs. This was obviously a sacred area, and shows that the Goddess continued to be a central part of the worship of these Postpalatial (Mycenean) people.

Snake tube

Returning to the road, it continues down to the small village of **PACHIA AMMOS**, with several tavernas along the sea front. Recent excavations have shown that the area was probably used as a harbour for Gournia, and on headlands to the west of the village were found store rooms, a wharf, a ship shed, fortifications and a dam across the river. On a hill slope above a cove between the headlands (directly below the site) a Neopalatial [LMI] cemetery

Beach at Pachia Ammos

was excavated in 1910 by Richard Seagar, and in 1914 a substantial Neopalatial cemetery was exposed on the beach at Pachia Ammos after a severe storm. Finds included six larnakes (burial chests) and 200 pithos burials.

From Pachia Ammos, there is a choice of two major routes. One road continues eastwards towards Sitea. For details of sites eastwards to Sitea and beyond, turn to p.94. The other route heads southwards towards Irepetra, through a natural valley between mountains, that would have been used in prehistoric times as a route between the north and south parts of the island at its narrowest point. Traces of Postpalatial [LMIIIC] refuge settlements have been found on the slopes of the mountains on the east side of this corridor, a lower one at **HALASMENOS** (where a sanctuary containing fragments of GUA figurines and snake tubes has been found) and a higher one at **KATALEIMATA**. On the western side of the corridor a substantial Prepalatial site has been found at Vasiliki. It is signposted off this Pachia Ammos to Irepetra road, about 3km inland from Pachia Ammos.

VASILIKI

Vasiliki was founded as a settlement site in the Prepalatial [EMII] period, when it consisted of houses that were crammed together in a communal way on the side of the hill. It is from this site and this period that the distinctive pottery, known as Vasiliki ware *[see box on p.10]* was found. Five sherds of pre-Vasiliki ware pottery, decorated with dolphins, was also found. The

settlement reached its peak in the Protopalatrial [MMIB] period, but continued into the Neopalatial [LMI] period and beyond.

The complex has two separate buildings, named the West House and (to the east of the site) the Red House, so named from the red lime plaster used to cover the walls. The site also has a paved area, to the west of the West Court, which looks like an early version of what was later to develop into the central courts of the palace-temple sites. In the south-east corner of the site is a baetyl stone *[see box on p.58]*, a sacred stone that was venerated as a representation of the Goddess. It has been recently suggested that its placing here was deliberate, to create a view of a cave in the mountains on the opposite side of the valley. Something like the shape of this baetyl

Baetyl stone

is depicted on a gold ring from **Phourni** tholos tomb A, which shows an adorant hugging such a stone on the left of the scene, while a priestess occupies centre stage, with the epiphany *[see p.18]* also indicated by two butterflies descending.

KEPHALA VASILIKI

On a neighbouring hill to the west of Vasiliki (and visible from the site) a Postpalatial site [LMIIIC] has recently been excavated. In the southern wing of the complex were found three rooms that had been used for the storage of cult equipment associated with a room where was found a baetyl *[see box on p.58]* laid out on an altar. In a nearby shrine room *[see box on p.98]* were found fragments of five, possibly six, Goddess with Upraised Arms figurines (one of which is in **Agios Nikolaos musem**). One of these was uniquely enthroned. Although this site is much later in time than **Vasiliki**, the location of a baetyl at each site shows the continuity of the tradition, and in this case emphasises the association of a baetyl stone with Goddess objects used for ritual purposes.

Continuing south along this road, it goes past (on the western side) the village of **EPISKOPI**, where were found chamber tombs of the Postpalatial [LMIII] period, including a fine painted larnax, now in **Irepetra museum** *[see below]*. On the eastern side is the village of **KATO HORIO** where was found the magnificent Neolithic Goddess figurine, now in **Heraklion Museum** *[see photo on p.9]*. Arriving in **Irepetra**, there is a small archaeological museum.

IREPETRA

The Museum is open daily (except Mondays) 08.30 - 15.00 and contains finds from nearby sites, including Goddess (GUA) figurines and snake tubes from **Kavousi** and **Vronda**. There is is also a beautifully decorated larnax *[right]* from **Episkopi**, painted with 12 panels including a chariot procession and a stylised octupus, with the gable of the lid depicting a bull's head at one end and a human figure at the other. From the Graeco-Roman city state of Hirepetra comes a 2ndC CE marble statue of Demeter, with a sheaf of corn and snakes headdress.

From Irepetra there are important Minoan sites to the east (Makriyalos) and the west (Phourni Korphi and Pyrgos) of the town.

MAKRIYALOS

At Makriyalos (25km east of Irepetra) there is an important Neopalatial [LMIB] house a 'manorial villa' that controlled agriculture and fishing in the area. It was constructed like a palace-temple site in miniature, oriented north-south and has a central court (exactly four times smaller than the main sites), colonnades, and remains of a west court. There is a large altar at the northern end of the central court (opposite the west entrance), and facing it a bench that was doubtless used for ceremonies. Here was found a seal showing a sacred boat bearing a priestess making an adoration gesture, in front of a palm tree and a wooden altar *[drawing right]*. Also found was a bronze Goddess figurine with pronounced breasts and genitals, sherds of Marine style pottery, and a large stone anchor which the excavator, Kostas Davaras, thought was a votive offering to a Minoan Sea Goddess. The house was destroyed in the 1450 BCE conflagration.

From Makriyalos, you can journey north to **Sitea** to visit the sites around that area *[see p100-104]*, but for this section, we return to **Irepetra** to travel westwards along the south coast. About 3.5km along the road heading westwards is the village of **GRY LYGIA**, where was found a burial site 1km north of the village at Arape. Two Postpalatial [LMIII] rock-cut chamber tombs with dromoses (entrance walkways) have been excavated, and found within were larnakes and accompanying grave goods of pottery, bronze tools, weapons and jewellery. The painted horns of consecration, *[see box on p.15]* now in **Aghios Nikolaos musem** *[see p.85]* came from this site, and shows that Minoan sacred symbols still had significance and power in this later (Mycenean) period.

The road continues westwards until it reaches the village of Myrtos. Just before the village there are two important Minoan sites, **Phourni Korphi** and **Pyrgos**.

PHOURNI KORPHI

Phourni Korphi is the first site reached, 1.5km from Myrtos, on the right hand side of the road, at the top of a gulley. It is also an extremely difficult site to get to: there is no proper path, and access to it involves a hair-raising scramble on uneven ground up the side of the gulley. It is however an important site. It was founded in the Prepalatial [EMII] period, and, like **Vasiliki** from the same period, it consisted of a number (in this case about 90) densely packed small rooms and passages.

From Phourni Korphi looking towards Pyrgos

Here was established a thriving community of about six family units, living and working together. Material discovered at the site included evidence for the cultivation of cereals, olives and vines, and the herding of sheep, goats, cattle and pigs. There was equipment for weaving and pottery, and for the making of wine and olive oil. The past seems very alive here. If you can gain acess to the site (it is usually locked) then there is a real feel of the everyday life of the people, with pestle and mortars (used for grinding spices and herbs), quern stones (used for crushing grain), and decorated bowls still lying about. However, as is usual at nearly all Minoan sites, the everyday lived side by side with the sacred, for in the south-western corner of the site, archaeologists found a shrine *[see box on p.98]*, one of the earliest yet known to the Minoan Goddess. Here was found a clay figurine of a Goddess, holding a miniature jug, which can now be seen in the **Aghios Nikolaos musem** *[photo on p.84]*. The village was destroyed by fire in about 2200 BCE, and sadly was not rebuilt.

PYRGOS

Just before the turning into Myrtos, there is a second site on a hilltop, to the right of the road. Pyrgos is easier to get to, though it still involves a steep climb up the side of the hill. The original site dates to the same Prepalatial [EMII] period as the neighbouring **Phourni Korphi** site. It is in a dramatic position, with beautiful views to the south over the sea, and to the north over the mountains *[see photos right and front cover]*. It was destroyed at the same time as Phourni Korphi (around 2200 BCE), but unlike the former site, Pyrgos was rebuilt, and continued into the Neopalatial [LMI] period. During this period an elegant two or three storey house was built on the summit of the hill, the lower storey of which remains today. There was a great appreciation of beauty incorporated into the building, such as the use of gypsum and ashlar masonry, and deliberate use of colour contrasts in the floors and courtyard. Some of this is still visible today, including a beautiful pathway of flagstones in purple limestone leading towards the sea. At the southern corner of the site, is a column base with an edging of purple limestone, which indicates where a small shrine would have been located. Near the staircase there were also signs of a shrine from an upper floor having fallen in. Finds included a Linear A tablet, two clay sealings, a conch shell of pink faience and four clay tubular stands for

offerings. On the NW side of the hill, remains of a two-storey communal tomb can still be seen. This is a site where the love of beauty and spirituality by the Minoan people can be best appreciated.

From Myrtos, the road turns inland to head for Ano Vianos, which is in Heraklion Province, and from where it is possible to either head back northwards to **Heraklion,** or to continue westwards to visit **Phaistos** and **Aghia Triada** *[see p.64-70]* and the tholos tombs of the **Mesara Plain** *[see p.71-76]*. Along the road, some 10km west of Myrtos (just into Heraklion Province) you reach the village of Kato Pefkos. Here, take a small right hand turn that leads up into the hills to the village of **Kato Symi**. Through the village, the road becomes a dirt track that takes a series of hairpin bends up to the (fenced) Sanctuary of Hermes and Aphrodite.

KATO SYMI – Sanctuary of Hermes & Aphrodite

This sanctuary or temple site was a place of worship from the Protopalatial period to the 3rdC CE. In the Neopalatial period, this was an open air sanctuary with a paved approach road, and would have been a pilgrimage centre where the Minoan people would have travelled to worship the Goddess and ask for her blessings. A large number of stone offering tables (many  inscribed with Linear A script *[see box on p.12]*) have been found here, together with many votive offerings, including stone vases and clay and bronze figurines. From the Postpalatial period, three bronze swords with incised decoration were found. In later Hellenistic and Roman times, the sanctuary became dedicated to the god Hermes and the goddess Aphrodite, as evidenced by markings on a house shrine and votive offerings, including a 7thC BCE enthroned female. It has been suggested that the Hermes and Aphrodite names became attached to this place because of memory of the site being dedicated in Minoan times to the Goddess and her consort.

This completes the section from Aghios Nikolaos to Irepetra. We now return to **Pachia Ammos** *[p.88]* for the section from Pachia Ammos to Sitea.

FROM PACHIA AMMOS TO SITEA

The road from Pachia Ammos arrives first at the village of Kavousi, from where it is possible to visit a number of sites in the mountains to the south, in particular **Azorias, Vronda** and **Kastro**. It is possible to drive the first part of the route, as far as "the oldest olive tree in Crete" (which has been dated as far back as the Postpalatial period of Minoan Crete), but from there the route gets increasingly rough, and should only be attempted by four-wheel drive or on foot.

The first site to be reached is the post-Minoan site of **AZORIAS**, situated on a hill with two peaks *[see photo on p.95]*. The site was originally occupied in the Neolithic period, but the remains to be seen today date from the Archaic Period (7th - 5th century BCE). In the centre of the settlement archaeologists have revealed public buildings, storerooms, a temple, and the alleys leading to the central court, the agora. There was a shrine, that contained an altar on which were found a variety of terracotta votive female figurines, votive stands and vessels, and food offerings. The inhabitants cultivated the surrounding slopes and valleys with olives, vines, cereals, and were also engaged in fishing, farming and pottery.

VRONDA

There was a site here in the Late Neolithic and Prepalatial periods, but what remains is a sizeable settlement from the Postpalatial [LMIII] period. On the ridge there is a large building with a court, where was found a stone kernos *[see box on p.57]* with 24 circular depressions set in an oval ring. On the SW slope of the ridge, a shrine building was found with benches around the sides. Over 30 GUAs (Goddesses with Upraised Arms) and fragments of GUAs *[see box on p.23]* were found here. Also found were 17 nearly complete snake tubes and seven kalathoi (offering bowls), one decorated with horns of consecration *[see box on p.15]* and another with inscribed snakes inside it. This was clearly a place that had a strong element of Goddess worship.

On the north slope below the site were a number of small tholos tombs *[see p.71]*, and the site itself was re-used in the Late Geometric period [8thC BCE] as a cemetery.

KASTRO

From Vronda retrace your steps to Ayia Paraskevi
church for the path that climbs steeply to Kastro,
about 45 minutes walk upwards to a height of
710m. This was a refuge settlement, originally
dating from the end of the Postpalatial [LMIIIC]
period and into the Late Geometric period [8th-
7thC BCE]. It was built in a precipitous position
on the side of a towering peak, with houses
occupying narrow terraces around the pinnacle,
and subsequently spread across the saddle of the
mountain to the eastern slopes. It is something of
a mystery as to why this site was built in such a
remote and inaccessible location, with no fresh
water nearby. The finds from the excavations here
include Goddess figurines, with stumpy arms and

*View of Azorias
from Kastro*

emphasised vulvas. They are quite crudely made and unpainted.A stone kernos
[see box on p.57] was also found, providing a link to earlier Minoan sites.

PSEIRA

Returning to Kavousi, the main road
now climbs eastwards to panoramic
views over the coast to the island of
Pseira, which was occupied in Minoan
times. It was founded in the Prepalatial
[EMI] period and developed to a town
of some 60 houses, built in terraces on
a sheltered peninsula in the SE side
of the island, overlooking a natural
harbour and away from the prevailing winds. There was also a town shrine,
where fragments of moulded plaster were identified by the excavator as being the
remains of a Goddess. Some remains of frescos were also found, some showing
seated Minoan women. There are striking similarities between this building and
a MM II shrine at **Malia**. Both structures had an unusual arrangement for entry
to the building, a single large room on the west side and an area for religious
practices on the east side. A very impressive tall, steep flight of steps, known
as the Grand Staircase, leads up from the beach to the town, which was divided
by the archaeologists into four separate areas. There was a town square and a
possible courtyard in one of the areas, that was used as a work area. The site was
destroyed at the end of the Neopalatial period during the 1450BCE conflagration.

MOCHLOS

A turning off the main road leads to the harbour of Mochlos, with a number of tavernas arranged picturesquely around the harbour. Off shore is an island (which may be visited by private boat hire from the mainland), that was joined to the mainland in Minoan times by a narrow isthmus. On the island was an extensive Prepalatial [EMII to MMIA] cemetery and a Neopalatial town. The cemetery, on the western end of the island, is the largest and most important Prepalatial cemetery in eastern Crete, and consisted of two rock shelter tombs *[photo right below]* and some 26 house tombs built into the cliffs. Outside the tombs was a paved area with an outdoor shrine.

Many burial offerings were found in the tombs, evidencing a cult of the dead *[see box on p.47]* including a lot of gold jewellery (It has been calculated that over 40% of all the individual gold items and 50% of the value of all the gold found in Early Minoan Crete deposits come from Mochlos alone). There were also seal stones (one of which was a silver cylinder seal from Mesopotamia), silver cups, faience, diadems, and one of the finest collections of stone vases in Minoan Crete, made of rock crystal, marble, steatite and brecchia. One of these vases was the Goddess of Mochlos libation jug *[photo right and on p.10]*. One burial jar had incised double axes *[see box on p.14]* picked out in white dots, and a gold signet ring *[photo below]* was also found, portraying a Goddess sitting in a boat with a horse-head bow and stern of a fish, that is similar in some ways to the sealstone found at **Makriyalos** *[see p.90]*. It has been interpreted as a kind of epiphany scene, whereby the Goddess arrives at a site to bless it with her presence.

96

Below the cemetery, evidence has been found of a Prepalatial settlement, that was eventually replaced (on the south side of the island) with a Neopalatial town, that may have been settled by incomers. The largest three-storey building, which was probably the administrative centre, had pillar crypts *[see box on p.37]* on the lowest floor. Finds included the head of a female figurine. Also, during excavations in 2009, part of a collapsed wall was found, under which was a pyxis (small circular stone box) that depicted an unusual scene of a Goddess epiphany, whereby a couple are being presented to the Goddess.

Some of the tombs in the Prepalatial cemetery were also re-used in the Neopalatial period.

On the mainland opposite *[photo right]*, around the modern village, evidence of a Postpalatial [LMII] settlement (with tombs) has been excavated. It had a bench shrine and workshops for the production of brass artefacts, stone vases, pottery and oil production. This settlement was destroyed in the 1450BCE conflagration, but Mochlos remains a major centre for evidence of Minoan civilisation and culture.

MYRSINI

Returning to the main road, after a few kms you arrive at the village of Myrsini. North of the village, on a hill by the sea, 12 rock cut tombs of the Postpalatial period were excavated in the 1960s. Grave goods included a rich variety of vases, weapons and utensils now on show in **Agios Nikolaos museum**, including an adorant female figurine on a drum base *[photo on p.85]*.

On the slopes below Myrsini is a much earlier, circular tholos tomb, the first (and one of the few) of the type from **Mesara** to be found in eastern Crete. It contained over 60 burials dated by the associated finds to the end of the Prepalatial era.

The road continues through **MESA MOULINA**, where two tholos tombs from the Postpalatial [LMIII] period were discovered. Rich grave offerings included a gold mask, bronze vessels, and a Mycenean-type sword. The tombs were later re-used in the ProtoGeometric period [10thC BCE].

Continuing towards Sitea, the road now passes by a large lay-by on your right hand side (signposted), from where you can walk to the Minoan house of **Hamezi**.

HAMEZI

A 10-15 min walk leads from the main road to the late Prepalatial site of Hamezi, located on the top of a knoll, with spectacular views over the Bay of Sitea. Originally, there were a number of square and rectangular buildings on the top of the knoll, but towards the end of the Prepalatial period these were built over with the oval shaped building, the remains of which can now be seen.

This oval shape is unique in Minoan architecture, and seems to have been built deliberately in that way. At the centre of the site is a courtyard with a circular cistern that provided water for the inhabitants, and the rooms are arranged around this central feature. One room in the NE side of the building has been identified as the shrine

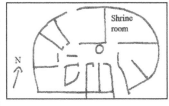

room *[see box below]*, for it was here that parts of a clay altar, offering table, rhyta (libation jugs) and three complete figurines (and fragments of several others) were found, similar to the kind of votive offerings often found at Peak Sanctuaries *[see box on p.16]*. There is a direct view to surrounding hills from the site, which have distinctive shapes, including twin hills that look like breasts and between them the shape of a 'sleeping Goddess' in the land.

The main road now leads into the town of Sitea, that is built around the harbour.

DOMESTIC/HOUSE SHRINES. As well as the Shrine Areas and Dining Shrines in the Palace-Temple sites *[see box on p.67]*, most private houses and villas seem to have had their own shrines, as an integral part of the house. They were built as early as the Prepalatial period, as in the example from **Hamezi** *[above]* and **Phourni Korphi**, and continued throughout the Protopalatial [see for example **Apodoulou**], the Neopalatial [see for example **Vathypetro** and **Amnisos**], and continued into the Postpalatial period [see for example the shrine rooms at **Gournia** and **Kephala Vasiliki**]. They usually consisted of a single room with a bench running along one wall for the deposition of cult images, votive offerings and Goddess figurines. Scholars have debated as to whether they were intended for use by everyone in the house or only a select few (the elite) but it seems that they represent the same kind of central part that the Goddess played in the lives of everyone in Minoan Crete, in both Palace-Temples and houses alike.

SITEA ARCHAEOLOGICAL MUSEUM

Open: Daily (except Mondays) 0830 to 1500
Location: Beside the main road going southwards towards Makriyalos.

There is a good selection of finds from sites in eastern Crete. From the Neolithic cave of **Pelekita** near Zakros there are stone axes. Then there are examples of pottery from the Prepalatial cemetery of **Aghia Photia** near Sitea, followed by finds of votive offerings from Peak Sanctuaries *[see p.16]* in the area, especially **Petsophas**. From **Mochlos** and **Pseira** come stone vases, some in the Marine Style of decoration; and there are also finds from the recent excavations at **Petras**. Finally, from **Roussolakkos at Palaikastro**, and the palace-temple site of **Zakros** come rhyta (libation vessels), pots and basins and spouted jars.

Many examples of ritual objects are included, such as lamps and stone offering tables, horns of consecration, double-axe stands and kernos vessels *[photo below]*. There are a number of pots that are most interesting, as they appear to show a butterfly symbol metamorphosing into an early double axe shape *[see photos right]*. There are also several large pithoi, one of which shows a large double-axe decoration *[photo below]*. Finally, there is the restored statuette (one quarter life size) of a kouros (male figure) made from chryselephantine, that was discovered at **Roussolakkos at Palaikastro**. It has been suggested that it may represent a Boy God, companion to the Minoan Goddess, but no one is certain. It was clearly controversial at the time, as it was deliberately vandalised when the site was destroyed in the 1450 BCE conflagration.

*Finds on display in
Sitea Museum*

SOUTH OF SITEA

to Aghios Nikolaos
N
Sitea
to Zakros
× Manares villa
Piskokefalo
to Achladia
× villa
× tholos tomb
Zou villa
Zou
Epano Episkopi
× Agios Georgios villa
× Praisos
Nea Praisos
to Makriyalos

Taking the road going south from Sitea towards Makriyalos (and on to Irepetra), there are a number of Minoan sites.

MANARES (KLIMATARIA)

The road cuts through the remains of this Neopalatial [LMIA] villa, that was originally terraced into the hillside, but whose eastern lower part has now been destroyed. A staircase at the northern end of the site gave access to the upper levels. Sherds of pottery and parts of pithoi were found during the excavations, and below the modern road, the excavators found a room with a small pillar, that may have been a pillar crypt *[see box on p.37]*.

ZOU

One km further south the road reaches the village of Piskokefalo. From here, on the left (east) a minor road leads through Kato Episkopi to a large Neopalatial [MMIIIB] building on the hillside before the village of Zou. The building originally had about 20 rooms, that included the domestic quarters and rooms for the storage of grain. A small room with a bench suggested a domestic shrine *[see box on p.98]*, and there was also a possible ceramics kiln. Finds included pithoi, pots, amphorae, bowls and jugs; some bridge-spouted jugs were decorated with double axes.

ACHLADIA – House

Returning to the main road through the village of Piskokefalo, there is a signpost on the right (west) for Achladia. One km along this road (before the village of Achladia), on the left hand side of the road are the remains of a large Neopalatial [MMIII] villa, covering an area of 270 sq metres. The main house had 12 rooms, that included a polythyron (or pier and door) partition, that was typical of Palace-Temple sites. Many vessels of a domestic use were recovered from the site, though there was little evidence of items of a religious nature.

ACHLADIA - Tholos tomb

From the Minoan house, a rough road (paved for the first part) leads on for about 1 km to a sign that points to a path through an olive grove, that leads to the Achladia tholos tomb. This a Postpalatial [LMIIIB] tholos tomb *[see box on p.71]* that is in an excellent state of preservation. As you approach the tomb, there are the remains of buildings that may have housed the priest/esses who attended the tomb and oversaw the arrangements for the 'cult of the dead' *[see box on p.47]*. The tomb itself is approached by a long dromos (passageway) leading to a rectangular entrance door. Inside, there is a circular chamber built of large stones towards a corbelled roof. Opposite the entrance there is a small doorway, that leads to an inner chamber. Originally this was blocked by two walls, forming a false entrance, that was probably designed for the spirits of the dead to move into the afterlife.

Although the tomb had been robbed prior to its excavation during World War II, nevertheless three larnakes (clay coffins) remained, all decorated with sacred symbols of the Goddess. One was decorated with a double axe *[see box on p.14]*, horns of consecration *[see box on p.15]* and a griffin *[see box below]*. The lid of another larnax was shaped like the back of a bull, with the head and tail at the gable ends, showing the significance of the bull cult continuing into this period.

North of the village of Achladia, at **LAPSANARI**, terracotta votives and some pottery were found, including seven plaques of a naked female, who may represent a Goddess, and one of a sphinx. The site probably dates from the Archaic-Hellenistic periods [7th-1st century BCE], the same as **Praisos**.

THE GRIFFIN The iconography of the griffin (with the body of a lion and the head of an eagle), as depicted on Minoan sealstones, rings and frescos, is a complex but important one. At **Knossos** in the Throne Room *[see p.38]* a restored fresco depicts griffins guarding the throne of the Priestess; in **Knossos** in the Great East Hall *[see p.28]* a fresco pictured griffins tethered to columns; at the burial site of **Phourni** in a crypt *[see p.46]* a gold ring was found depicting a goddess and a griffin; and on the **Aghia Triada** sarcophagus *[see p.24]* two goddesses are depicted travelling in a chariot drawn by griffins. It seems to represent both a guardian of a sacred place, and/or protection and connection to Goddess or a Priestess. The symbol remained in use throughout the Palatial and Postpalatial periods.

AGIOS GEORGIOS

Returning to the main road at Piskokefalo, it continues south for about 5km until it reaches Epano Episkopi. A minor road to the left (going south) winds its way to the village of Agios Georgios. Before it arrives there, another minor road turns right to a hilltop crowned with yet another Neopalatial villa. This one was built on four terraces, with the upper  parts having survived. The quality of construction was excellent, built with large limestone blocks, and staircases between the four levels. On the top terrace were storerooms, grape-pressing equipment, millstones and a potter's wheel. On the second terrace, there were loom weights from weaving looms, and rooms that the excavator thought were used primarily by the women of the house. The villa, like the others in the area, was probably destroyed in the 1450BCE conflagration.

PRAISOS

From Agios Georgios, return to the road from Epano Episkopi and continue along it to the village of Nea Praisos. From here, take a track heading northwards that eventually leads to the hilltop site of Praisos. Traces have been found of Neolithic use (in a cave 500m north of the site), and evidence of Minoan activity (at a Neopalatial building 800m SE of the hills, Postpalatial chamber tombs 200m SE, and a GUA from that period [LMIIIC] found nearby at Kapia). The site itself consists of three hills (known as the First, Second & Third Acropolis), and was founded right at the end of the Minoan  period by people who were probably escaping from the incoming Dorians. They are thought of as EteoCretans (true or original Cretans), as they used a Greek alphabet but in a pre-Greek language, that was most probably descended from Minoan Linear A script *[see box on p.12]*. The First Acropolis hill has remains of a temple; on the side of the Second Acropolis there are remains of houses; and the Third Acropolis (a flat-topped wedge shape hill) had an altar with rock-cut steps and a Sanctuary. Female figurines were also found here. The site thrived during the Archaic and Hellenistic periods [7th to 1st centuries BCE].

From Praisos return to the main road, south to Makriyalos *[see p.90]*, or north to return to Sitea.

EAST OF SITEA

PETRAS

Heading east out of Sitea, the first major turning on the right (south) leads up to the Minoan settlement site of Petras. This is a complex site, begun in the Prepalatial [EMII] period. Some Vasiliki ware *[see box on p.10]* was found from this period. In the Protopalatial [MMIIA] period, the plataeau was levelled and work on a kind of Palace-Temple site began. There was a Central Court, oriented N-S, a monumental staircase, and a room where hieroglyphic documents were stored. Kamares ware pottery has been found. Three rooms have been excavated, one of which is thought to be a shrine *[see box on p.98]*. At the end of this period the site was destroyed (perhaps by the earthquake in 1700 BCE), but in the Neopalatial [MMIII] the Palace-Temple style building was reconstructed, with a Central Court, and (as in the other Palace-Temples) rooms on the west side, which probably served as cult places, as indicated by a libation table and tablets of Linear A script found there. This central building was surrounded by other smaller buildings (two of which have been excavated) which consisted of living rooms, storerooms and workshops. The site was abandoned at the beginning of the Late Minoan period following violent destruction, and only partially reoccupied during the Postpalatial period.

Returning to the main road, a short distance further on, at the headland, there are the remains of the Hellenistic [4th-1stC BCE] town of **TRYPITOS**. There were coins, pottery and jewellery found here. Less than 1km further on, again on the seaward side, there is the cemetery of **Aghia Photia**.

AGHIA PHOTIA

This Prepalatial [EMIB] cemetery of Aghia Photia is the largest Minoan cemetery so far found in Crete. A total of 252 graves were discovered, with at least another 50 having been destroyed by cultivation of the surrounding land. The graves are of an early chamber tomb type, with an ante-chamber and main chamber, and there are also simple pit tombs which probably  contained child burials. Almost all the tombs had more than one burial. A number of tall cups with pedestals were found in some of the antechambers, associated with the 'cult of the dead' *[see box on p.47]*. There were many other finds, including about 1800 vessels of various types all in excellent condition, as well as stone and bronze objects, many of which show there was regular contact with the Cyclades *[see box below]*. Nearby a large stone rectangular building was found, dating to MMI, that had 37 rooms, with an elongated central court or corridor linking the rooms. It was abandoned after a short period, and two tholos tombs were built on top of it about 200 years later.

MINOAN CONTACTS. From the earliest Prepalatial period, Crete had peaceful contacts with other parts of the Aegean which were already flourishing, such as the Cycladic islands. Some pots exported from Crete have been found in the Cyclades, and conversely, characteristic Cycladic Goddess figurines have been found at Minoan sites. For example 15 figurines found at **Phourni** [Tomb C] were of this type. By the end of this period, Crete had established relations with the Syro-Phoenician coast and Egypt, where imported Minoan objects have been found. Crete also traded with Cyprus, from where they obtained copper for the making of bronze, and on at least two Cycladic islands, Milos and Kythera, they established colonies. By the Neopalatial period there were also Minoan settlements and colonies on a dozen or so Aegean islands, the largest and most important of which was Thera (Santorini), which may have been equal with Crete as a Minoan centre. Kythera was also important: from here, Minoan influence spread to the south Peleponese, and on Kythera Minoan tombs and a Peak Sanctuary have been discovered. There is also record of rich gifts brought from Crete to Egypt; and there would also have been extensive contact between the Minoans on Crete and the Myceneans on the mainland, which may have led to the Mycenean invasion in the Postpalatial period. Perhaps it was because the Myceneans had absorbed Minoan Goddess-worship that they brought it back again.

ROUSSOLAKKOS at PALAIKASTRO

The road running eastwards eventually arrives at Palaikastro from where there are signs for the Minoan settlement at Roussolakkos. This lies on a flat plain beside the coast, with views one way to a flat-topped hill (Kastri), and the other to the Peak Sanctuary hill of **Petsophas** *[photo right]*.

On Kastri, there is evidence of walls dating from both the Prepalatial [EMIII] and Postpalatial [LMIIIC] periods, and at the site of Roussolakkos itself there was evidence of occupation from the Neolithic to end of the Postpalatial period and beyond. The town developed in the Protopalatial and Neopalatial periods, and, although destroyed in the 1450BCE conflagration, it was rebuilt in the Postpalatial era and became the largest town in eastern Crete, with a sheltered harbour and a fertile hinterland. There is no central building (or court), but rather a number of blocks of houses and buildings, which are mapped out on interpretation boards at the site. In each block, there was a Hall, in the majority of which there were lustral basins *[see box on p.38]*. Building 1, which was constructed in the Neopalatial [LMIA] period, was a shrine or temple, and just outside the building was found a carved statuette with a head of serpentine and eyes of rock crystal.

Evidence of cult activity was found throughout the site and on an extensive scale. Among the finds of a religious or cult nature were incense burners, rhyta, triton shells, large stone baetyls, horns of consecration *[see box on p.15]* and double axes *[see box on p.14]*. There were also many finds of Goddess and other figurines. For example in House ß (room 5) three female figurines of clay, the clay head of an ox and marine style sherds were found. In House D (room 44) Postpalatial [LM IIIA] vases plus clay objects connected with the cult of a Snake Goddess were found. These included four female figurines dressed in long skirts: on three of the figures, the arms, though broken, were originally outstretched while the fourth held a striped snake in her arms. *[see p.19]*. Also found were clay doves that had probably been perching on a trinity of sacred altars. In House N (room 19) a Postpalatial [LMIII] Goddess figurine *[drawing right]* was discovered on a recess to a larger room. Finally, in a separate area the Kouros *[photo on p.99]* was discovered: a unique piece that has no parallel anywhere else in the Minoan world.

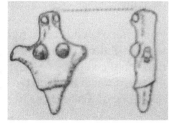

PETSOPHAS

Petsophas Peak Sanctuary *[see box on p.16]* was established during the Protopalatial [MMIB] era of the town of **Roussolakkos** which lay below it. It continued in use until the end of the Neopalatial [LMI] period, and was during its use an extremely well-visited site. It lies to the south of Roussolakkos, and can be reached by returning from the Minoan town towards Palaikastro, and then turning off left to the suburb of Angathias, outside of which a path runs to the top of the 217m high hill. As you approach the summit of the hill, colourful purple limestone indicates the approach to the sanctuary. Tucked against the rocks on the

Petsophas Peak Sanctuary (foreground)

summit, the walled sanctuary contained a small shrine with benches. A great quantity of votive offerings was found, including human and animal representations in clay, horns of consecration *[see box on p.15, p.84 and drawing right]* and stone offering tables, inscribed in Linear A script *[see box on p.12]*. The animal figurines included tortoises, hedgehogs and weasels, which Paola Pugsley suggests may have represented a cult of the Minoan Goddess as Mistress of the Animals.

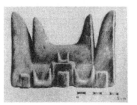

From Palaikastro, there is a choice of routes. A road north of the town leads to the far NE peninsula (also approachable by a turning off the main eastern road over a hill by Mount Toplou Monastry) . This comes down to the coast again at Vai, with its palmtree forest. North of Vai are the bays of **ITANOS**. There was a Neopalatial house here, but it was not until Graeco-Roman times [7th-5thC BCE] that it became one of the most important city states in eastern Crete. At least four temples are recorded from Classical times. There was rivalry between it and neighbouring **Praisos**, and subsequently **Hirepetra**. On the nearby headland of Cape Sideros, there was a temple to the Goddess Athena Samonia in the Classical or Hellenistic [4thC BCE] period. Some remains of what may have been the temple can sometimes be seen below the sea off the point of the Cape.

From Itanos, you can return to Palaikastro, and take the road going south towards **Zakros**, which weaves its way across a bleak but spectacular mountain range to the villages of Langada and Hohlakies. About 3km south of this latter village, a rough track on the left (east) side leads up to another Peak Sanctuary – this one of **Traostalos**.

TRAOSTALOS

There is not a great deal to see at Traostalos Peak Sanctuary, other than the view over Zakros Bay, but in Minoan times it was an important Peak Sanctuary, presumably visited by the inhabitants of **Zakros** in the same way as Petsophas was visited by the inhabitants of **Roussolakkos**. At 515m it was more than twice the height of Petsophas, and the two Peak Sanctuaries were intervisible. It was excavated in 1963-4 and finds included ceramic boats, stone altars, stone discs and clay figurines of animals and humans. The animal figurines included bulls, goats/sheep, birds, fish and beetles. Five bronze female and male figurines were discovered, and a clay one that was naked with the pubic triangle shown. As at the other Peak Sanctuaries, these would have been offerings to the Goddess.

Continuing on the road going south, it arrives at the town of Ano (upper) Zakros. From here a pathway leads to the **GORGE OF THE DEAD,** a 6km walk that goes down to the Palace-Temple site of **Zakros**. The early part of the walk just outside the town cuts through a Neopalatial [LMI] country house, where a wine press and a pithos inscribed in Linear A *[see box on p.12]* were found. The path through the gorge can also be accessed further along the main road (signposted) that leads directly into the Gorge and shortens the way somewhat. The Gorge is

so named from the caves in the rocks on the lower part that were used in the Prepalatial [EM & MM] period for burials.

The bottom of the gorge flattens out to the site of Zakros, with its Palace-Temple, the neighbouring Minoan town, and what would have originally been the harbour.

MINOAN HARBOURS Minoan Crete had a number of safe harbours where ships could be breached on stretches of sand, and some elementary harbour structures also existed. The principal harbour for the Palace-Temple site of **Knossos** was Katsambas, for **Phaistos** it was nearby **Kommos**, and for ancient **Hania** it was Souda Bay. Other places, for example **Mochlos**, had their own harbours, which were instrumental in the growth and development of the sites. It was the ease of landing on Crete that brought people to the island in the first place (stone tools found in SW Crete have been dated to at least 130,000 years ago) and it was the availability of harbours that allowed the Minoan people to establish trading links with other places *[see 'Minoan Contacts' on p.104].*

ZAKROS

Open: April - end Oct, Daily 0800-1900. Nov - Apr, Daily 0800-1500
Location: 34km from Sitea, 20km from Palaikastro.
Summary: Zakos is the smallest of the Palace-Temple sites, but has the remains of a substantial terraced town attached to its northern end. It is an atmospheric site to visit, with the advantage of a few tavernas nearby along the water's edge for rest and refreshment after visiting the site.

History of Zakros

Zakros Palace-Temple probably arose here because of its sheltered position for a harbour *[see box on p.107]*, and its location at the end of the Gorge of the Dead. Zakros was inhabited in the **Prepalatial** period when the town grew up, and then the first Palace-Temple was built in the **Protopalatial** period. There was a Central Court on the current NE-SW axis, which is different from the other Palace-Temple sites, and also a West Wing. The site was destroyed in the 1450BCE conflagration,

Looking across the Central Court to the terraced town behind

but was quickly rebuilt, and it is the remains of the **Neopalatial** [LMI] site that can be seen now. It covers an area of 8000 sq. mtrs and had 150 rooms. The site was never looted, so the range of finds when excavated was impressive.

Tour of Zakros

The site is entered from the south (1) leading into the Central Court, which measures 30m x 12m, about one third of the size of the Central Court at **Knossos**. There is the stump of an **altar** (2) in the northern part of the Court, similar to the ones at **Knossos** and **Malia**. Also similar to all the other Palace-Temple sites, the west wing of Zakros is the area devoted to the buildings put aside for ceremonies and the storage of cult objects. There was a **pillar crypt** (3) *[see box on p.37]* and the so-called **Hall of Ceremonies** (4) with central columns and polythyron (pier-and-door) partition walls. It had relief frescos and decorative panelling, and in a **light-well** (5) next to the Hall were found the bulls head rhyton *[picture right]* and the 'Sanctuary rhyton' *[see details on p.110]*.

108

Plan of Zakros

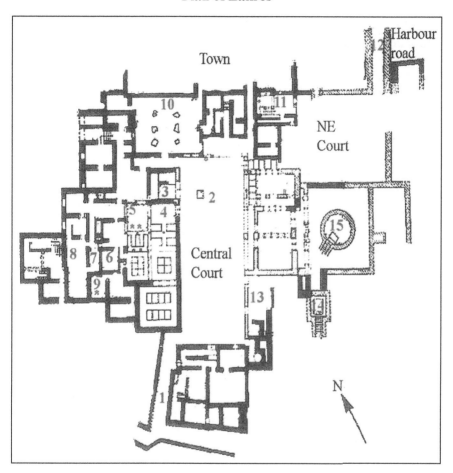

1. South entrance
2. Altar
3. Pillar crypt
4. Hall of Ceremonies
5. Light well
6. Lustral basin
7. Central shrine
8. Archives room
9. Treasury
10. Kitchen / Dining room
11. Lustral basin

12. North entrance
13. Unit of the built well
14. Well of the fountain
15. Cistern room

** Finds of Bulls Head rhyton and
   Sanctuary rhyton (in 5. Lightwell
   at Hall of Ceremonies)
* Find of rock crystal rhyton
  (in 9. Treasury)

109

The 'Sanctuary' (or 'Mountain Shrine') rhyton *[drawing right]*, although damaged by fire, is a beautifully decorated vessel that depicts the scene at a Minoan Peak Sanctuary *[see box on p.16]*. At the bottom are the horns of consecration *[see box on p.15]* from a tripartite shrine, and above this the shrine door, on top of which sit four wild goats. Around the side of the rhyton are depicted more wild goats and horns of consecration.

Further to the SW of the light-well lie three rooms next to each other. Room (6) was a **lustral basin** *[see box on p.38]*; room (7) was a central **shrine** that may have been a Dining Shrine *[see box. on p.67]*. This was a small room with two benches and finds of libation vases. Room (8) was the **archives room** where record tablets, some inscribed in Linear A *[see box on p.12]* were kept. To the south of these rooms was the **treasury** (9) where eight clay chests full of vases and pots were found. These included the beautiful rock-cut crystal rhyton, now in Heraklion Muesum *[see picture on p.20]*, together with other vases, chalices, mace-heads, bronze double axes *[see box on p.14]* and artefacts in ivory and faience. This room had not been plundered, so was able to give a vivid picture of the beauty and wealth of Minoan craftsmanship.

Moving to the north side of the site, there is a large room (10) that was originally a kitchen, with a dining hall above. Next to this was another **lustral basin** (11) (now roofed). Remains of frescos were found here, showing sacred objects like double axes and horns of consecration. This area marked the **north entrance** (12) to the site, and the road from the Minoan harbour led directly to this entrance.

On the east side of the site were various wells and springs, some of which contained offering cups and dishes, and which now are frequently flooded in winter and are the abode of turtles. This completes the tour of the site, although to the direct north of it are the extensive remains of the terraced town, abutting directly on to it. Town and Palace-Temple must have had a close and intimate relationship with each other at this site.

From the site, a path leads north to the **PELEKITA CAVE** *[see box on p.63]*, about 5km from Zakros, involving an hour's walking, or 15mins by boat. It is about 310m in length, and has a number of large rooms with a rich array of stalactites and stalagmites. Traces of Neolithic habitation have been found here, including a limestone Neolithic idol, which is in **Aghios Nikolaos museum**.

This concludes the section on Eastern Crete.

WESTERN CRETE [Rethymnon province] – map

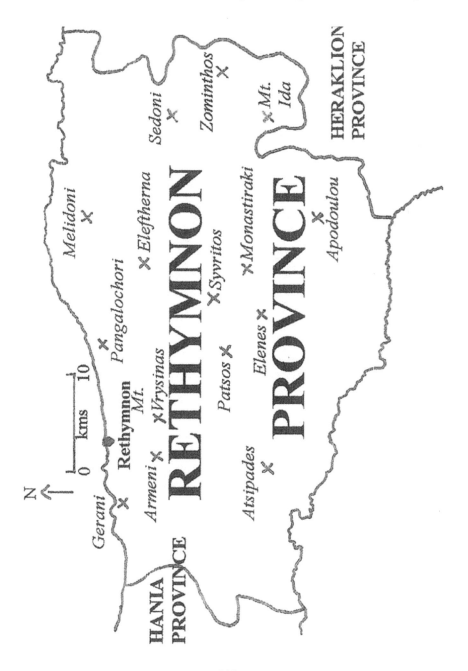

WESTERN CRETE
[Province of Rethymnon]

Western Crete is much less endowed with Minoan sites. Why that should be is something of a mystery, but it does seem that the focus of much Minoan occupation and activity was in the central and eastern parts of the island. However, that is not to say that there are no Minoan sites in the west: in Rethymnon province there is the important Palace-Temple type site of Monastiraki, the settlement at Zominthos, Postpalatial cemetery at Armeni, two important Peak Sanctuaries at Vrysinas and Atsipades, a sanctuary at Patsos, and sacred caves at Mt. Ida, Kamares, Sedoni and Melidoni, as well as some later City States.

FROM HERAKLION TO RETHYMNON

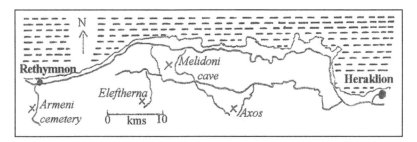

From **Heraklion** take the National Highway west towards **Rethymnon**. After about 70km take a turning south for the **CAVE OF MELIDONI** (entrance fee), which was used from Late Neolithic to Roman times. Although initially used as a place of residence, the cave became a place of worship during the Middle Minoan period [2100 - 1600 BCE], and a copper axe was found here as well as large quantities of pottery. In Classical times it became a sanctuary dedicated to Hermes Talaios, a giant who was believed to have protected the island of Crete. In 1824, 250 Greeks were massacred here by suffocation by the Turks.

From here, continue south-east towards Zoniana for the City State of **AXOS**. The site was first occupied in the Postpalatial period, on a saddle between two hills with a steep acropolis to the south. It was developed into a City State in the Archaic and Hellenistic periods, where a temple to Aphrodite crowned the top of the hill, and many votive offerings were found. Just south of Axos is the **CAVE OF SEDONI** (entrance fee and guided tour). This is a quite spectacular cave, where evidence of activity from Neolithic to Roman times has been found. From Zoniana travel east to Anogeia and then 5km south to **Zominthos**.

ZOMINTHOS

Zominthos (fenced and not open) is a large Neopalatial settlement [LMIA], dated approx 1600 BCE, with traces of an earlier settlement found under its NW wing. It is located about 1,200 metres above sea level on a level plain, and lies on the ancient route between **Knossos** and the sacred **Mt. Ida**. It is the largest Minoan country house ever found, covering an area of 1600 sq. mtrs. and part of a larger settlement site of

at least 3000 sq. mtrs. The house was oriented north-south, like the palace-temple sites, and had 2 storeys and over 50 rooms. The central building is well preserved, and was decorated with wall paintings. There was a ceramic workshop (remains of more than 250 vessels were found) as well as a potter's wheel, together with bronze tools and rocks of quartz crystal. Other finds that indicated a sacred use were rhyta, a beaker jug, a bronze cup and three incense burners. There were also finds of an adorant figurine, and sealstones showing a scorpion and a lion. The site was destroyed by an earthquake and fire, perhaps in the 1450 BCE conflagration.

Mt. IDA – IDEAN CAVE

South of Zominthos, reached by a mountain road, lies Mount Ida, a scared mountain on whose summit lies one of the most important and well visited caves *[see box on p.63]* in Minoan Crete, lasting from the Neolithic until Roman times. When excavated, it yielded a huge quantity and quality of finds, together with traces of burnt animal bones and ash, associated with sacrifices and ritual meals. Finds from the Minoan periods (Prepalatial to Postpalatial) included terracotta and bronze figurines, wine jugs and basins, together with numerous objects in gold and ivory. From later periods, such as the Geometric, came a large number of bronze tripod cauldrons, and from

the Orientalising period came ceremonial bronze shields. The site has legendary connections to Zeus, though before that it must have been a sacred place for Goddess worship. On the southern flanks of Mt.Ida lies the **Kamares Cave** (in Heraklion Province), reached by a steep climb of 4-5 hrs from Kamares village. Large quantities of Kamares ware pottery *[see box on p.10]* and some animal figurines and other deposits from the Protopalatial period were found here.

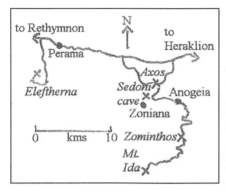

to Rethymnon
N
to Heraklion
Perama
Axos
Eleftherna
Sedoni
cave
Anogeia
Zoniana
0   kms   10 Zominthos
Mt.
Ida

ELEFTHERNA

SW of Melidoni, through the village of Perama, lies the Dorian City State of Eleftherna. Once again, the site was already in use in the Prepalatial [EM] period, with some figurines found that show evience of contact with the Cyclades islands *[see box on p.104]*. But it was from the Geometric and Archaic periods [9thC BCE onwards] that it developed as a City State, the same period as **Lato** and **Dreros** *[see p.82]*. There was a sanctuary and cemetery here (where human and animal figurines were found), and in Roman times a Temple dedicated to Hermes and Aphrodite. A statue of Aphrodite was found, and fragments of a statue of a Kore (female figure), also from the same period.

In recent years, excavations have focussed around the Orthi Petra necropolis on the site, and the remains of four females, ranging in age from seven to seventy, were excavated in an 8thC BCE monumental funerary building. Artefacts recovered from the tomb included bronze vessels and figurines, gold jewellery, a stone altar, ritual bronze saws and knives, and a rare glass phial for pouring libations. All this suggests that the women played an important role in

Eleftherna's religious life, and the site director believes that the oldest one was a High Priestess interred with her protégés, all of whom were related to her in some way. This matrilinear 'clan of Priestesses' would have occupied a prominent place for several centuries. Two especially interesting pendants were recovered from the site. In 2009 a pendant was found, depicting a Goddess with Egyptian features and either pots or bees on her chest *[photo right above]*. And in 2010 a female skeleton was found that was wrapped in more than 3000 pieces of gold foil that would originally have been part of a robe or shroud. There were other grave goods, including pottery, perfume bottles, amber, crystal and faience beads, and the pendant *[photo right below]* that was probably part of a rock crystal and gold necklace, and which also resembles a bee Goddess. If there was a cult of the Bee Goddess at this site, this would have links with the Bee Goddess pendant found at **Chrysolakkos** at **Malia** *[see p.11 & 60]*, although that dates from a much earlier period.

Returning to the village of Perama, about 8km to the west is the small village of Viranepiskopi with Ano (upper) **VIRANEPISKOPI** church to its south. The church is now in a ruined state, but originally there was a temple to the Goddess Diktynna here. This Goddess was found mainly in western Crete *[see p.130]*, with a variant of her, Britomartis, found mainly in the east *[see **Skotineo cave** on p.54 and **Hersonisou** on p.55]*. Both Goddesses may be localised versions of the Goddess Artemis.

West of Viranepiskopi is the small village of **PANGALOCHORI** where a tholos tomb was excavated, and a GUA (Goddess with Upraised Arms) figurine *[see box on p.23 and photo right]*, dating from the Postpalatial period, was found. The figurine is now in the Rethymnon Museum.

Arriving in **RETHYMNON**, the contemporary town stands on the site of the City State of Rethymne or Rithimna. Initially the city was fairly insignificant, but it slowly began to flourish, minting its own coins, and being the centre for the worship of the Goddess Rokia Diana, who was the patron deity for those bitten by rabid dogs!

RETHYMNON ARCHAEOLOGICAL MUSEUM

Open: Daily (except Mondays) 0830-1500
Location: Opposite the main gate of the Venetian fortress, close to the Harbour.

The Museum is housed in one large room, with the exhibits arranged in a clockwise direction, in chronological order, from the earliest on the left of the entrance.

The first section starts with prehistoric / Neolithic material from cult cave sites at **Melidoni, Gerani** and **Maryieles (Elenes)**. This is followed by finds from the Prepalatial and Protopalatial periods. These include a clay model of a sanctuary and a stone kernos *[see box on p.57]* from the settlement at **Monastiraki**; and figurines of worshippers and animals, and a stone altar with Linear A inscription *[see box on p.12]* from **Mt. Vrysinas** Peak Sanctuary. There are also finds from the **Apodoulou** site. From the Postpalatial period, there are finds from the Mastabas area of **Rethymnon**; from the tholos tomb at **Pangalochori** *[photo above]*; and from the cemetery of **Armeni**, which yielded a good amount of grave offerings, including a boars tusk helmet.

There are also decorated larnakes (clay burial chests) from **Armeni**, depicting octopus, bulls, bears and wild goats in a ritualised hunting scene, together with painted double axe *[see box on p.14]*, horns of consecration *[see box on p.15]* and tree-of-life motifs. Then there are finds from the City State of **Eleftherna** and the cemetery at Orthi Petra, and finally material from the Classical, Hellenistic and Roman periods, including a number of statues from Roman sites of Stavromenos and Lappa. One of these is of Aphrodite, and another of Artemis *[photo right]*, who was the Greek and Roman equivalent of the late Minoan Goddess Diktynna/Britomartis.

SOUTH OF RETHYMNON

From Rethymnon, there are two main roads heading south, one directly south that goes past the cemetery of **Armeni**, and one to the east of the city that goes in a SE direction through the picturesque Amari valley to the village of Thronos, above which lies the ruins of the late Minoan Refuge site and later City State of **SYVRITOS**. The site dates from the 12thC BCE [LMIIIC], making it contemporary with **Karphi** and **Kastro** in the East. On the acropolis (hilltop) remains have been found of a monumental building, a section of paved road and ruined houses.

AGHIAS ANTONIUS SANCTUARY (PATSOS)

To the west of Thronos and **Syvritos** is a minor road that leads to the base of the Agh. Antonius gorge and dam, near the village of Patsos. At the base of the dam, a sign directs you to the sanctuary in the gorge, at the entrance of which is the cave and Chapel of Agh. Antonius. This open-air Sanctuary has been in use since Late Minoan times, similar to the one in the East of the island at **Kato Symi**.

A stream runs through the gorge, and there are pools, rock shelters and pathways in this delightful spot. Finds from the Late Minoan period include bronze figurines of worshippers and animals, offering tables, a double axe *[see box on p.14]* and horns of consecration *[see box on p.15]*. The site continued in use throughout the Hellenistic and Roman periods, when it was dedicated to Hermes Kranaios, and into the Christian period as well. An interpretative plaque at the site suggests that the Hermes dedication

Cave & chapel (above) stream (below)

took over from the Minoan cult of "the fertility of nature, the feelings inspired by the changing of the seasons, and the mystery of the vegetation cycle".

MONASTIRAKI

Returning to the main road at Agh. Fotini, continue south for 4km, and visible to the right (west) is the Minoan settlement of Monastiraki. To reach the site, turn off outside the small town of Agh. Fotini, or further south at the village of Platania for the village of Monastiraki. On a lower road of the village there is informal parking, and then a short walk down a steep hill to the site that lies on a slope in the bottom of a valley. The site is fenced, but at the time of writing was open to the public under the watchful eye of a village guardian, who will permit no photographs to be taken. This is partly because the site is still under excavation, and only limited excavation reports have been published. It is, however, evident that this was a major Minoan site, that covered a huge 300,000 sq. metres, and is considered to have characteristics that are similar to the other Palace-Temple sites. Current thinking is that it was a satellite area to the site at **Phaistos** that lies some distance away to the south.

The site dates from the Protopalatial [MMII] period, and, following the earthquake and fire at the end of that period [c.1700 BCE], was never rebuilt in the Neopalatial period. This makes it unique as a site that came to its end before the New Palace-Temples were constructed, and therefore provides an insight into Protopalatial architecture and construction that was not built over (though there was some limited reoccupation at the end of the Postpalatial [LMIIIC] period). Three separate areas have been excavated, and finds have included much pottery and sealstones. On the western side (originally excavated by German archaeologists in WWII) a Minoan Hall with a central column and two courts was found. On the southern side, a miniature clay shrine was found with horns of consecration *[see box on p.15]*. On the eastern side, some 90

(Above) location of the site (below) the excavations [Credit: Archaiologia]

interconnecting rooms, storerooms and workshops have been uncovered. Two rooms produced evidence for ritual activity. In a rocky outcrop (known as Kokkinos Charakas) a large number of conical cups were found indicating cult activity, together with a unique figurine, dating from the Postpalatial [LMII] period. The figurine shows what appears to be a naked woman suckling a young male adult. It has been suggested that this is a representation of the Minoan Mother Goddess giving succour to her divine consort, though nothing like it has been found at any other site.

About 6km to the west of Monastiraki at the village of Elenes lies the **MARYIELES** cave, where a not dissimilar groups of attached figurines have been discovered. The figurines were originally attached to a clay plaque, and are in a fragmentary condition. Nevertheless, an attempted reconstruction by archaeologists has suggested that one of the figures at least was a Goddess. Also found in the cave were stone vases, including a goblet that could have been used for ritual libations, and some sherds from ritual vases. All of this suggests that the cave was used for cult purposes, probably by people from Monastiraki, to celebrate and worship the Minoan Goddess.

Returning to **Rethymnon**, take the road running due south to Spili. About 8km south of the city, lies the Postpalatial [LMIII] cemetery of Armeni.

ARMENI CEMETERY

This is the biggest Postpalatial cemetery of its kind in Crete, with 231 tombs, including one tholos *[see box on p.71]* having been uncovered up until the present time. Initially high and low status tombs were kept separate, but this was soon abandoned, as more tombs continued to be added, each one probably representing a family group. The tombs were all cut into the rock, which is quite

hard, which has helped to preserve them. They are built in two distinct styles: in the first there is a large tomb with a long dromos (entrance passage) and steps leading down from ground level; and in the second type there is a small tomb with a short dromos and no steps, or no dromos and a few steps. Each tomb was sealed with a large slab of stone. There were three types of chamber: circular, semi-circular, and in the case of the most prestigious tombs, rectangular, with a low bench along one or more walls. The most imposing tomb (no.159) had a dromos of 15.5 metres and a staircase with 25 steps, and was 2.45 metres in diameter.

Inside the tombs the dead were buried in larnakes (clay coffins), many of which were elaborately decorated with classic Minoan sacred symbols of double axes *[see box on p.14]* and horns of consecration *[see box on p.15]*. Many of these can now be viewed in the **Rethymnon Archaeological Museum**. There were also offerings found in some of the tombs, including pottery, bronze vessels, tools, jewellery, stone vases and four cylindrical seals from the Middle East *[see box on p.104]*. A clay figure of a Goddess with striped body was found, and also a steatite pendant with Linear A inscription *[see box on p.12]* which predates the Postpalatial period, so may have been handed down as a family heirloom. One of the most unusual finds was a helmet made of 59 boars' tusks, which is now in the **Rethymnon Archaeological Museum**. A quantity of broken pots found on a paved area linked to a dromos by a channel were indicative of a cult area.

The bones of some 500 individuals recovered from the larnakes were analysed. They showed that life expectancy for men was only about 31 years, and for women 28 years. They ate a high carbohydrate diet but consumed little meat. For many years it was not clear where the people buried in the cemetery had lived, but recent research shows that there was probably a large settlement a few kms to the west, now buried under the present-day village of Kastellos.

MT. VRYSINAS PEAK SANCTUARY

One interesting feature of the tombs in the **Armeni cemetery** is that they are all oriented eastwards towards Mt. Vrysinas, which is visible from the site at 858 metres high. This was already a Minoan Peak Sanctuary from the Palatial period when Armeni cemetery was being built, so it shows that the Postpalatial people at Armeni had a reverence for their ancestors and their sacred mountain.

The Peak Sanctuary has yielded a great number of fragments of drinking cups (nearly 7000), over two dozen pithoi (storage vessels), a bull rhyton (libation vessel), and a rare stone altar with Linear A inscription. There were also many animal and fish votive offerings, and male and female bronze and clay figurines.

ATSIPADES KORAKIAS PEAK SANCTUARY

Western Crete has a lot less Peak Sanctuaries than the central and eastern parts of the island: in fact the only two that have been positively identified and excavated are **Mt. Vrysinas** *[above]* and, more recently, the one at Atsipades Korakias. This lies 12kms south of Mt. Vrysinas on a 983m hilltop above the village of Atsipades, and the two sanctuaries are intervisible. It was in use in the Prepalatial period [EMIII-

MMI], probably by people from a local rural community, as there is no evidence of any substantial Minoan town nearby. Finds from the site include spindle whorls for weaving, ceramic lamps, altars, cups and jars, several rhyta and numerous clay human and animal figurines. Many of the votive offerings had been deliberately placed in rock clefts, in the same manner as those on **Mt. Jucktas**.

WEST OF RETHYMNON

Returning to Rethymnon, there is just one site worth mentioning about 6km west of the city, just off the National Highway before it enters Hania province. This is the beach of **GERANI**, behind which is a cave that was used as a sanctuary in Neolithic times *[see box on p.63]*. Finds from the cave (including bone and obsidian tools) are displayed in the **Rethymnon Archaeological Museum**.

WESTERN CRETE [Hania province] – map

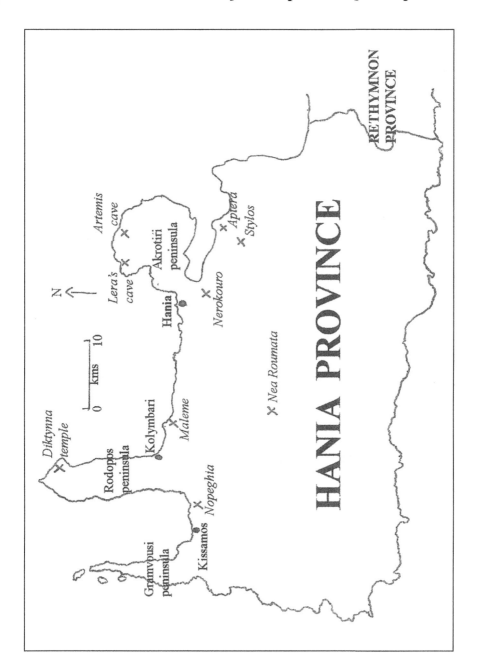

WESTERN CRETE
[Province of Hania]

Western Crete continues, and as we move further west the Minoan sites get even sparser. Here in Hania Province there are tholos and chamber tombs at Stylos, Maleme and Nea Roumata, but no large cemeteries; and there is a house at Nerokouro, and settlement sites at Stylos and (only recently excavated) at Trouilla, but no Minoan towns or large Palace-Temple sites. There are proportinally a great number of City States, but not much evidence of Goddess worship at most of them. However, we leave the best until last: the remote and inaccessible, but dramatic Temple to Diktynna at the very tip of the Rodopos Peninsula.

FROM RETHYMNON TO HANIA

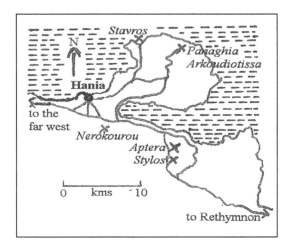

From Rethymnon take the National Highway going westwards for about 40km, and then turn off south to the City State of **APTERA**. This is an 8thC BCE site, which flourished in Hellenic times. The site was first excavated in 1942, and then in 1958, and a Temple was uncovered, dedicated to a pair of Goddesses, possibly Demeter and her daughter Kore. In the temple various examples of kernoses *[see box on p.57]* were discovered. Kernoses were used in Minoan times, and their use seems to have continued in the Hellenistic period, when they seem to have been particularly associated with Demeter, as the Goddess of agricultural rituals. A short distance away the remains of a Temple of Eileithyia, the Goddess of childbirth, were also found, who was also worshipped at caves near **Amnisos** and **Inatos**. Aptera was clearly a strongly Goddess-influenced site.

South of the City State of **Aptera** is an earlier Minoan settlement and tholos tomb, near the village of Stylos. This was probably called Aptera in Minoan times, as there is mention of it (as *a-pa-ta-wa*) in a Linear B tablet at Knossos. Travelling south, you come first to the tholos tomb, on the left (east) of the road.

STYLOS – Tholos Tomb

The tholos tomb is contemporary with the settlement and dates to the Postpalatial period [LMIII]. It is well preserved, with a dromos (entrance passage) 20.8 metres long and a vaulted circular chamber 4.3m in diameter and 4.8m high, that is still roofed. It was clearly an important structure, but sadly we shall never know who or what was desposited here, as the chamber was found looted with only a few potsherds left on the floor, though they were of good quality. The tomb is similar in style and construction to the tholos tomb at **Achladia** near Sitea, except that this one at Stylos has only one circular chamber without an inner one behind. During the 6th century BCE (Archaic period), a group of cups was deposited as a memorial offering on the upper part of the entrance to the chamber.

STYLOS – Settlement

Further south along the road, again on the left (east) side are the remains of the Postpalatial settlement. A 11m long wall was uncovered, that was part of a building that incorporated a natural cave, that may have served as a reservoir. Finds from

the building included sherds of pithoi, long-necked goblets, obsidian blades, grindstones, loomweights, spindle whorls and other items. There was also a masons mark (trident) on one of the walls. Nearby there were the remains of a circular ceramics kiln, dating to LM IIIB period. It is the only kiln from this period known in western Crete, and consists of three narrow elongated channels 1.3m long, of which the central channel is straight but the two side ones appear slightly curved following the general shape of the kiln. In 1972 another building consisting of an oval room and antechamber was discovered between the settlement and the tholos tomb. It is not known whether it was a house, a place of worship or used for some other social purpose.

NEROKOUROU

There is not much to see at the fenced site of this Neopalatial [MMIIIB] house, that lies just south of the National Highway between Souda and Mournies, but it was an important rescue excavation. The original settlement was quite extensive, with buildings grouped into neighbourhoods, but much of the site was destroyed by bulldozing before it could be excavated. What still remained included a central hall with paved floor, some evidence for storage activity, and an external paved courtyard using coloured slabs. Ceramic and stone tools were found, suggesting that food may have been processed and stored there. The site was destroyed in the 1450BCE conflagration. Subsequently, another Minoan building [MMIII-LMI] was discovered about 300m west of this site. It consisted of storage rooms, and finds included pithoi and ceramics.

HANIA & THE AKROTIRI PENINSULA

Arriving in **HANIA**, we have reached what was probably the 'missing' Palace-Temple site of the West. The reason that we do not have the remains of the site, as at **Knossos**, **Malia** and **Zakros** is that after its destruction (probably in the 1450BCE conflagration) it was reoccupied for a time in the Postpalatial period when it was known as **KYDONIA** (Linear B tablets from Knossos refer to it as *ku-do-ni-ja*). A City State then arose here, and continued into the Roman period and beyond. It is on top of all of this that the modern city stands. However, excavations on a low hill called Kastelli near the harbour front (at Ayia Aikaterini Square) have revealed that it was occupied from the beginning of the Prepalatial period through to the end of the Postpalatial. Remains of four or five houses were found with several rooms, some with frescos *[see box on p.26]* and paved entrances. A large cache of Linear A tablets *[see box on p.12]* was found, reinforcing the notion that this was a former Palace-Temple site. Further excavations in the City at Daskaloyanni Street have revealed a substantial Minoan settlement dating to to the Neopalatial period, where six rooms with a lustral basin *[see box on p.38]* and fescos were found.

The evidence for this being a Palace-Temple site falls into four categories. Firstly, there is the large number of Linear A tablets recovered, second only to those from **Knossos**. Secondly, many features present in the architecture of the other Palace-Temple sites have been noted here, including Minoan Halls with pier-and-door partitions, light wells, lustral basins, fresco paintings, columns, pillars and storage rooms. Thirdly, a number of ceremonial and cult areas have been identified; and finally, a number of seal impressions have been found, one of which depicts what may have been the Palace-Temple site itself. A complex of buildings is shown of several storeys, crowned with horns of consecration *[see box on p.15]* and a deity.

HANIA ARCHAEOLOGICAL MUSEUM

Open: Daily (except Mondays) 10.00-1700
Location: Situated in the former Venetian Monastery of Saint Francis at 25-30 Chalidon Street, opposite the main gate of the Venetian fortress, close to the Harbour. In 2008 it was announced that a new purpose-built Museum was to be constructed in the historic Chalepa area of the city, but with Greece's economic problems, it seems to have been put on hold for the present.

The eastern side of the Museum houses the Minoan material, while the western side houses the later exhibits. The collection starts with the late Neolithic, with hand axes, stone vases and obsidian blades from cave sites *[see box on p.63]*, followed by material from excavations in Hania town. From the Kastelli Hill excavations there is a clay sealing with a representation of a Minoan city and its patron deity, together with a clay tablet inscribed with Linear A script from the same site. There is also a clay pyxis (small lidded box) with a representation of a kithara player in a landscape with birds, found in a chamber tomb near the Kiliares river below **Aptera**. Material from the Postpalatial period, including pottery, vases, jewellery and seals, shows extensive trading activities between western Crete and the Mediterranean world.

From later periods finds are displayed that include early 9thC BCE [Geometric period] gold disks from a female pythos burial at Pelekapina near Hania; and

the head of a clay figurine from a female burial in a rock-cut tomb in Hania from end of 4thC BCE [Classical period]. The Museum also houses the Mitzotakis Collection with some beautiful (but unprovenanced) pieces, including clay figurines of bird-faced women (Goddesses?) from 600-575 BCE [Archaic period] *[photo right]*.

THE ARCHAIC GODDESS The post-Minoan period did not mean that all worship of (and representations of) the Goddess ceased. The Archaic, Classical and Hellenistic periods [600-67 BCE] saw the rise of the City States and the development of Sanctuaries, often dedicated to named Goddesses and Gods. Finds from the Archaic period include a terracotta plaque depicting in relief a female with upraised arms (survival of GUA motif), from Mathia, Pediada area *[see p.32]*; plaques of a naked female from **Lapsanari**, who may represent a Goddess *[see p.101]*; and the bird-faced Goddess/women illustrated above.

THE AKROTIRI PENINSULA

CAVE OF THE BEAR [ARTEMIS CAVE]

North of Hania lies the Akrotiri peninsula, where the airport serving Hania and the west is situated. At the northern edge of this peninsula lies 'the cave of the bear', or in Greek, the cave of Panaghia Arkoudiotissa. Take the road to the Monastry of Aghia Triada, and then the track northwards to the Gouverneto Monastery. Park here, and take a track down towards the ruins of Katholiko Monastery. After about 10 mins beside the path lies the cave *[see box on p.63]*. At the entrance is a small chapel dedicated to Panaghia Arkoudiotissa, which

is Greek for the Virgin of the Bear, a very thin Christian overlay for the Bear Goddess, who is venerated in the cave in the form of a huge stalagmite, which resembles a bear. The cave was dedicated to the Goddess Artemis, and here offerings were made to her in antiquity. This is one of the most powerful and sacred caves to the Goddess in the whole of Crete.

LERA'S CAVE AT STAVROS

Returning from the Cave of the Bear towards the Airport, take a minor road going NW to the resort of Stavros. Here in a sheltered cove is a cliff (known as Zorba's cliff after the film 'Zorba the Greek' that was made here), near the top of which can be seen a cave. This cave is known as Lera's cave, Lera being one of the Cretan nymphs. The cave was in use throughout the Minoan period into the Hellenistic, and finds from the cave are in the **Hania Archaeological Museum**. At the cave entrance are niches and polished spaces on the rocks for the placement of dedications and altars. One of the four rooms contained a body of water, in the vicinity of which large numbers of ceramic fragments belonging to the Archaic, Classsical and Hellenistic periods were found. In another room three stalagmites, which resemble veiled figures, were the focus of much sacrificial activity and dedications, including 55 terracotta statues of females, mainly of Classical date, holding a rectangular object or round bundle at chest level, which may denote a child.

CITY STATES IN WESTERN CRETE

In this far western part of Crete, there is a preponderance of City States dating from the Archaic, Classical and Hellenistic periods [650-67 BCE]. On or near the **south coast** these include:-

• ANOPOLIS (modern Anopoli), and its harbour PHOINIX (modern Loutro).
• TARA (modern Palaia Aghias Roumeli), in the Samarian Gorge, which was first inhabited in Minoan times and from where a stone column with a double axe *[see box on p.14]* is now in **Hania Archaeological Museum**.
• LISOS (near modern Sougia), where in Hellenistic times there was a Sanctuary and a temple dedicated to Asclepios, god of healing, and his daughter Hygieia, who was depicted with a sacred snake. Remains of the Asclepieion can still be seen, including a libation channel, which was the place of Hygieia's sacred snake.
• ELYROS (north of Lisos), which has never been excavated, and 5km to the west through Rodovani, HYRTAKINA, which had a Hellenistic sanctuary dedicated to Pan.
Near to the **north coast** there are two main sites:-
• PHALASAMA on the western side of the Gramvousa peninsula, which was occupied in Minoan times but became an important naval and commercial centre in the Hellenistic period. Finds are in the Museum in Kissamos.
• POLYRRHENIA, south of the town of Kissamos, was an Archaic and Hellenistic hilltop stronghold. Finds from its necropolis are in the Museum in Kissamos.

WEST OF HANIA

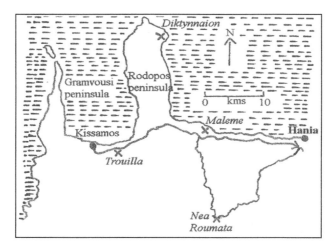

MALEME CHAMBERED TOMB

Take the National Highway from Hania for about 15km and then exit to the town of Gerani. From Gerani take the Old Road west for 3km to the resort of Maleme. To the west of the town on a hill lies the German War Cemetery (signposted). Drive up towards it, and before reaching the end, there is a signpost on the left pointing to the tomb. It is Postpalatial [LMIIIB] in date, and has a very long dromos (entrance passage) of 14m length.  The entrance is 2m high, with a recess above, and the tomb itself 4m high. When discovered, the tomb had already been looted, but two seals were found: one in bronze that may have been covered in gold leaf, showing a cow suckling her calf, and the other in agate showing a wild goat, both motifs associated with a Nature Goddess.

NEA ROUMATA THOLOS TOMB

Returning to the National Highway, take a minor road heading south for 14km to the mountain village of Nea Roumata. Just outside the village a small corbelled tholos tomb has been found, which is still in a good state of preservation. The tomb is early in date, from the Prepalatial [EMII] period, and was perhaps influenced by similar tombs in the Cycladic islands. The tomb *[illustrated below]* is very small, with a diameter of only 1.1m and a height of just 0.6m. It was built with river pebbles, and had contained a body in a contracted position, that was inserted from above. There were also two vases for grave goods, a spherical pot and a cylindrical cup placed  inside. Traces of another tholos tomb nearby were also found, and a third on the slopes of a hill 2km to the north at a place called Tomadalis.

Following the discovery, archaelogists investigated the surrounding low hills, and discovered walls of houses, dating to EMII and LMI periods. On a hill about 1km SE of the tomb they also found EM sherds of pottery, obsidian pieces and a piece of rock crystal. In another part of the same area there were also found stone pestles and clay spindle whorls. All this indicates that there was an Early Minoan habitation site here, from the time before the great Palace-Temple sites were built.

NOPEGHIA (TROULIA) SETTLEMENT

Returning to the National Highway, continue east (past the town of Kolymbari) for about 13km towards the town of Kissamos (Kastelli). About 3km before the town, on the south side of the National Highway, are the remains of recent excavations of a Minoan [EMII to LMIII] settlement. From the Protopalatial [MM] period, a villa was  excavated *[photo right]* with some remains of rooms and a surrounding wall to be seen. On a hilltop 200m SW, parts of two other buildings were found. To the south of the settlement, in the area of Aghios Dimitrios, an oblong pit from MMIIIB-LMIA was discovered dug into the bedrock, containing numerous vessels. It was thought that this was a ritual pit containing offerings to a deity, probably the Goddess. A Postpalatial [LMIIIA] elliptical building with a marked sloping floor was also discovered, that was probably used for religious practices. The site was abandoned at the end of the Postpalatial period.

THE DIKTYNNA TEMPLE

We have arrived at our final site – the Diktynna temple at the very edge of the Rodopos peninsula, one of the most remote and inaccessible places in the whole of Crete. It is not a Minoan site, but it was one of the most important religious sanctuaries in western Crete during the Hellenistic and Roman periods. Full details of the site and how to get to it are on the next page, but first, a look at who was the Goddess Diktynna.

> **DIKTYNNA.** The cult of the Cretan Goddess Diktynna in western Crete was related to that of Britomartis (a pre-Hellenic name meaning 'sweet maiden') in eastern Crete. Pat Cameron comments that "it was to some extent a survival of the worship of the Minoan mother goddess". The name Diktynna may be connected with Mt. Dickte (see the **Dictean cave** at Psychro), but the Greek historian Strabo proposed that *diktyon* was the fisherman's net which is supposed to have saved the goddess when she lept into the sea to escape the unwelcome attentions of Minos. Diktynna was a huntress and a Goddess of nature, the wild countryside and mountains. Her sanctuary was guarded by hounds which the Cretans claimed to be as strong as bears. There were also centres to her in Athens and the Peleponnese, and both Diktynna and Britomartis may have been localised versions of the Goddess Artemis, who continued to be venerated into historical times.

Diktynna's temple stands at the eastern point of the Rodopos peninsula, a long finger-like spur of land stretching 22km northwards from the town of Kolymbari. A minor road goes 5km north to the village of Rodopos, but beyond this there is only a very poor quality dirt track running north for 17km, with no dwellings or shelter anywhere along its length. Despite all the improvements to the Cretan road system, the Rodopos peninsula remains wild and remote. There are two possible ways of reaching it: one is by a boat from Kolymbari (there are occasional pleasure trips in the summer), and the other is by a four-wheeled drive vehicle by the dirt track from Rodopos. Contact Strata Tours in Kissamos to arrange this.

The remains of the temple itself lie above a sheltered (SE facing) cove, on a high promontary to the south of the cove *[photo right above]*. German archaeologists excavated here in 1943, only to find that the site had been systemetically looted and robbed. Originally it must have been a magnificent structure, a temple built of limestone, surrounded by columns using both blue and white marble, standing in a court paved in marble with stoas (collonaded porticos) on three sides *[drawing below]*. There was also a stepped altar of white marble, and beside this, at the south-west corner of the temple, there was a small circular building, where a statue of Diktynna with her hound was found (On display in **Hania Archaeological Museum**). The

temple was much visited by supplicants of Diktynna, and the rich offerings left to her were enough to fund the building of a Roman paved road that ran the length of the peninsula to the temple. Remains of this can be seen in places along the way, and a milestone from the road is still preserved in the village of

Rodopos. Only broken pieces of masonry and marble columns still remain, but one of these has the outline of the legs of a deer carved on it, an animal sacred to Diktynna. Despite its ruined state, this is an atmospheric place, and one that gives a flavour of the Goddess in Crete who was still worshipped and honoured here in the Hellenistic and Roman periods.

AFTERWORD

We have travelled through Crete from the centre to the furthest eastern part of the island and then to the furthest western part of the island, a journey of some 250+km in length. We have also travelled in time from the Neolithic period through the full flowering of the Minoan people and into the later times of the Archaic, Classical and Hellenistic periods – a journey through time of nearly 7000 years, a vast amount of time when you consider that it has only been 2000 years since then up to the present day. We have visited a large number of sites, well over 100 in total, including palace-temples, houses, villas, towns, mountains, peak sanctuaries, caves, harbours, cemeteries, tholos tombs, temples, refuge sites and city states. We have seen civilisations ebb and flow, as the Neolithic peoples turned into the Minoans, with their high level of civilisation and development, to be followed by the Mycenean incursions and later the EteoCretan people. In Museums and collections we have seen the finest examples of the craft skills and beautiful workmanship of these various peoples, as they expressed their love for the natural world. And running as a colourful thread through it all has been the Goddess, in many forms and manifestations, as the various peoples gave expression to the deity whom they felt watched over their lives and deaths, and gave them succour and meaning to their world.

Crete is not simply an amazing land that consists of a large number of prehistoric ruins and a collection of fine objects to admire. The spirit of the Goddess, that was so central to these people and their buildings and their beautiful objects, runs through the very fabric of the land itself, and is palpable today to anyone who visits the island with an open mind and an open heart. The ruins are not simply ruins: they are still alive with the spirit of the people who lived, worked and worshipped in them. The objects they produced are not simply Museum curiosities: they speak to us across the millennia with their love of beauty and celebration of the spiritual as well as the material. The history of this land and its peoples is not simply an entry in a book or a wall plaque in a Museum: it is in the very Mediterranean air, the warmth of the sun, and the feel of the soil that can still be experienced there today. Despite all the modern trappings of a society living in the 21st century, there is something about Crete that speaks to the modern pilgrim of a land and a people that is only just out of reach. The shadows of the ghosts of the Minoan ancestors still hover about the place, and sometimes at a site, when there is no-one else around, it feels as if you might turn a corner and find a Minoan woman or man, carrying herbs and spices, making beautiful objects, or singing, dancing and praising the Goddess. When that happens, you will know that the veil has dissolved and you have at last truly found the Minoan world and her Goddess.

BIBLIOGRAPHY

BOOKS

Branigan, Keith: "The Tombs of Mesara" [Ducksworth, 1970]
Cameron, Pat: "The Blue Guide to Crete" [A & C Black, 2003]
Castleden, Rodney: "The Knossos Labyrinth" [Routledge, 1990]
Castleden, Rodney: "Knossos: Temple of the Goddess" [Efstathiadas, 1997]
Crooks, Sam: "What are these Queer Stones? Baetyls:
    Epistemology of a Minoan Fetish" [BAR International, 2013]
Davaras, Costis: "Guide to Cretan Antiquities" [Eptalofos, 1976]
Davaras, Costis: "Gournia" [Hellenic Ministry of Culture, 1989]
Hughes, Dennis D: "Human sacrifice in ancient Greece" [Routledge, 2014]
Jones, Donald W: "Peak Sanctuaries and Scared Caves in Minoan Crete:
    comparison of artifacts" [Paul Forlag Astroms (1999)
Kanta, Athanasia: "Phaistos, Hagia Triadha, Gortyn" [Adam Editions, 1998]
Kyriakidis, Evangelos: "Ritual in the Bronze Age Aegean: The Minoan Peak
    Sanctuaries" [Duckworth, 2005]
Lapatin, Kenneth: "Mysteries of the Snake Goddess" [Da Capo Press, 2002]
Marinatos, Nanno: "Minoan Religion" [University of South Carolina Press, 1992]
Marinatos, Nanno: "Goddess and the Warrior: the Naked Goddess
    and Mistress of the Animals in early Greek religion" [Routledge, 2011]
Marinatos, Nanno: "Minoan Kingship and the Solar Goddess"
    [University of Illinois Press, 2013]
Moss, Marina: "The Minoan Pantheon" [BAR International, 2005]
(Ed.) Muhly, James D & Sikla, Evangelia: "Crete 2000: 100 years of American
    archaeological work in Crete" [American School of Classical Studies, 2000]
Panagiotakis, Georgios I: "The Dictaean Cave" [Panayiotakis, 1988]
Papadakis, Nikos: "Sitia" [District Council of Sitia, 1983]
Prent, Mieke: "Cretan Sanctuaries and Cults" [Brill, 2008]
Pugsley, Paola: "The Blue Guide to Crete [Somerset Books, 2010]
Sakellarakis, J & E: "Archanes" [Ekdotike Athenon, 2002]
Soles, Jeffrey S: "The Prepalatial cemeteries at Mochlos and Gournia"
    [American School of Classical Studies at Athens, 1992]
Vasilakis, Antonis: "Crete" [Mathioulakis, ?]
Vasilakis, Andonis: "Heraklion Archaeological Museum" [Adam Editions,?]
Vasilakis, Andonis: "Minoan Crete: from myth to history" [Adam Editions, 1999]
Vavouranakis, Giorgos: "Funerary Landscapes East of Lasithi, Crete in the
    Bronze Age" [BAR International, 2007]
(various) "From the Land of the Labyrinth: Minoan Crete 3000-1100 BC"
    [Alexander S. Onassis Public Benefit Foundation, 2008]

ARTICLES

Chryssoulaki, Stella: "The Traostalos Peak Sanctuary: aspects of spatial organisation [Aegaeum, 22, 2001]

D'Agata, Anna Lucia: "Religion, Society and Ethnicity on Crete at the end of the late Bronze Age. The contextual framework of LMIIIC cult activities" [Aegaeum, 22, 2001]

Dietrich, Bernard C: "Death and Afterlife in Minoan Religion" [Kernos, 10, 1997]

Driessen, Jan: "Crisis Cults on Minoan Crete" [Aegaeum, 22, 2001]

Gesell, Geraldine C: "The function of the plaque in the shrines of the Goddess with Upraised Hands" [Aegaeum, 22, 2001]

Goodison, Lucy: "From Tholos Tomb to Throne Room: perceptions of the sun in Minoan ritual" [Aegaeum, 22, 2001]

Jones, Bernice: "The Minoan 'Snake Goddess': new interpretations of her costume and identity" [Aegaeum, 22, 2001]

Kanta, Athanasia & Tzigouraki, Anastasia: "The character of the Minoan Goddess: new evidence from the area of Amari" [Aegaeum, 22, 2001]

Koehl, Robert B: "The 'sacred marriage' in Minoan religion and ritual" [Aegaeum, 22, 2001]

Nowicki, Krzysztof: "Minoan Peak Sanctuaries: reassessing their origins" [Aegaeum, 22, 2001]

Peatfield, Alan: "Divinity and performance on Minoan Peak Sanctuaries" [Aegaeum, 22, 2001]

Soles, Jeffrey S: "Reverence for dead ancestors in prehistoric Crete" [Aegaeum, 22, 2001]

Tsipopoulou, Metaxia: "A new Late Minoan IIIC shrine at Halasmenos, East Crete" [Aegaeum, 22, 2001]

Tyree, E.Leota: "Diachronic changes in Minoan Cave Cult" [Aegaeum, 22, 2001]

WEB SITE www.minoancrete.com

PICTURE CREDITS

All photos, maps and illustrations [c] the authors and Goddess Alive! (www.goddessalive.co.uk), except those on the following pages, which are reproduced under public domain and creative commons permissions: 4, 9 (Goddess), 18, 33, 49, 69, 84, 85, 86, 88 (snake tube), 95 (Azorias), 99 (kouros), 108 (rhyton), 114, 115, 118 [credit Archaiologia], 125 & 128 [permission obtained from photographer]. Wherever possible, we have attempted to source copyright holders, but if we have inadvertently omitted a creditation please let us know.

MAPS & PLANS

INDEX OF NAMED GODDESSES

MOTHER GODDESS. It seems likely that the Minoan people had a Mother Goddess. Recent decipherment of the Phaistos Disc claims to have identified a prayer to the Mother Goddess *[see p.13]*, and Greek history and mythology has a named Mother Goddess, Rhea, who may well date back to Minoan times. There was a Classical temple to her at **Phaistos**, and the **Dicktean cave** has a legend that Rhea gave birth there at midwinter to her divine child Zeus. She was the daughter of the Earth Goddess Gaia and the Sky God Uranus, and her name may mean 'flow' referring to her nursing milk that formed the Milky Way.

MOON GODDESSES. Greek mythology has a specific Cretan dimension to it. The Cretan-born god Zeus abducted Europa and coupled with her in the guise of a bull *[see p.28]* at Mitropolianos plane-tree at Gortyn. From their union came three sons, the eldest of which was Minos, who married Pasiphae, the daughter of the sun god Helios, and probably a moon goddess herself *[for more on Pasiphae see box on p.41]*. Here we have a clue to a lost matrilinear family of Moon Goddesses on Crete, beginning with TELEPHASSA, the mother of Europa whose name means "she who shines from afar". Her daughter, EUROPA's name means "with broad shining forehead", again an allusion to the moon. Europa's son Minos married PASIPHAE, whose name means "she who shines on all". Their daughter was called PHAIDRA (sister of Ariadne), who was the grandaughter of Europa, and whose name means "she who shines". Minos and Pasiphae also had a son Catreus, whose daughter was called AEROPE, who was therefore the niece of Phaidra, the grandaughter of Pasiphae and the great grandaughter of Europa. Her name means "she who shines in the air". Therefore, we have 5 generations of mythological women, all of whom have a connection to the moon, and all of whom may be the remants of a line of Moon Goddesses.

GENERAL INDEX

Entries in **bold** denote principal information. Entries in *italics* denote pictures.

137

Lightning Source UK Ltd.
Milton Keynes UK
UKOW06f0819150515

251535UK00022B/71/P